A Companion to
PHILEMON

CASCADE COMPANIONS

The Christian theological tradition provides an embarrassment of riches: from scripture to modern scholarship, we are blessed with a vast and complex theological inheritance. And yet this feast of traditional riches is too frequently inaccessible to the general reader.

The Cascade Companions series addresses the challenge by publishing books that combine academic rigor with broad appeal and readability. They aim to introduce nonspecialist readers to that vital storehouse of authors, documents, themes, histories, arguments, and movements that comprise this heritage with brief yet compelling volumes.

TITLES IN THIS SERIES:

A Companion to
PHILEMON

LEWIS BROGDON

CASCADE *Books* · Eugene, Oregon

A COMPANION TO PHILEMON

Cascade Companions

Cascade Books
An Imprint of Wipf and Stock Publishers
199 W. 8th Ave., Suite 3
Eugene, OR 97401

www.wipfandstock.com

PAPERBACK ISBN: 978-1-4982-9099-9
HARDCOVER ISBN: 978-1-4982-9101-9
EBOOK ISBN: 978-1-4982-9100-2

Cataloguing-in-Publication data:

Names: Brogdon, Lewis, author.

Title: A companion to Philemon / by Lewis Brogdon.

Description: Eugene, OR : Cascade Books, 2018 | Cascade Companions | Includes bibliographical references.

Identifiers: ISBN 978-1-4982-9099-9 (paperback) | ISBN 978-1-4982-9101-9 (hardcover) | ISBN 978-1-4982-9100-2 (ebook)

Subjects: LCSH: Bible. Philemon—Criticism, interpretation, etc. | Bible. Philemon—Commentary.

Classification: LCC BS2765.3 B7 2018 (print) | LCC BS2675.3 (ebook)

Manufactured in the U.S.A.

I want to dedicate this project to my New Testament professors from Louisville Seminary, Susan Garrett and Marion Soards. You fueled my love of the New Testament and taught me to handle the text with both care and creativity. It means so much to have you lend your incredible insights to this study of Philemon. I also want to express my gratitude to great colleagues who read and offered editorial suggestions and endorsements that were incredibly helpful as I pushed to finish this book while juggling heavy teaching and administrative responsibilities. Special thanks to Shannon Craigo-Snell, Tyler Mayfield, Amy Pauw, Love Sechrest, Emerson Powery, Otis Moss III, Amanda Brack, and Jill Bennett for taking valuable time to help me with this project. God has truly been good to me.

Contents

Foreword

DR. LEWIS BROGDON HAS devoted much of his life, personal and professional, to the study of Paul's brief letter to Philemon. He has had eyes to see what so many others have been unable to see, namely, the true treasure that is to be found in this very personal, but never private, letter from the Apostle Paul to his beloved coworker in Christ, Philemon. Through much of Dr. Brogdon's work I have had the privilege and the pleasure to observe, to interact with, and to learn from him as he pursued with passion his research and writing on Paul's letter. Now, it is my distinct honor to be able to say a few words at the outset of this book.

Brogdon has engaged the twenty-five verses of Paul's letter with constant care. He has searched high and low in a painstaking manner for the work of others who have studied and written about Paul's letter to Philemon. And, having sought out these scholarly contributions to the study of the letter, Brogdon has engaged the surprising range of pertinent ways in which careful students of Paul's writings have attended to linguistic, rhetorical, historical, sociological, theological, and exegetical interpretive considerations. Fortunately for his readers, Brogdon wears his learning lightly and is gifted at making murky matters clearer than they might otherwise be.

Brogdon alerts his readers to unknown, underappreciated, little understood, misunderstood, and misused aspects of the biblical text. Even when it has been studied with seeming care, Philemon, like so much other biblical material, has been employed as the screen on which many interpreters through the ages have projected their own assumptions, prejudices, programs, and all sorts of additional claims, especially theological.

Brogdon lures his readers into the study of Philemon by identifying several of the striking issues of interpretation that puzzle and divide both biblical scholars and other students of the Bible who are concerned to read, understand, and perhaps to bring some of their learning into daily life. He presents some of the history of the interpretation of Philemon. He identifies both strengths and weaknesses in these established traditional understandings. He takes his readers back to the earliest times in which Philemon was read, interpreted, and put to use in life by scholars, preachers, and teachers. These early Christian authorities employed Philemon to inform and persuade others about what those others should or should not do. Brogdon comments on this history of interpretation, pointing out the roles in which the letter to Philemon was cause for good and, perhaps more often, for something otherwise.

In this process of study Brogdon's readers become keenly aware of the genuine problems in the interpretation of this letter. His readers are helped to see a range of possible ways of understanding such puzzling obstacles to accurate comprehension of Paul's remarks. Brogdon points out the difference between the believable and the unbelievable, the likely and the unlikely, the persuasive and the problematic, and in all, he helps his readers to see what is impossible, improbable, possible, and probable for the understanding of the biblical text. It becomes apparent that all proposed interpretations must fall somewhere on this spectrum.

Brogdon joins a select group of other scholars in putting up a reasonable and responsible challenge to the age-old contention of many interpreters that is at the heart of the letter to Philemon, that which focuses and motivates Paul's writing is the problem resulting from a slave named Onesimus running away from the household of his master. Moreover, from verse 18 of the letter, many established interpreters suggest that Onesimus may have stolen something to cover the cost of his flight. Indeed, Paul's letter addresses a prominent person, a leader in the early church in whose house an early Christian congregation met, a man named Philemon, who certainly seems to be Onesimus's master. Paul's letter to this man concerns Onesimus. From the letter one learns that at the time he absconded from Philemon, Onesimus was not a Christian. Yet, one also learns that Onesimus had come (somehow) into Paul's presence—Paul is in jail (somewhere), though clearly Onesimus is not—and through Paul's ministry Onesimus had become a Christian. Paul writes this letter, obviously sending Onesimus and the letter back to Philemon. Paul explicitly writes on Onesimus's behalf, intervening with Philemon to call on him to receive Onesimus without harshness, not merely as a slave, but as a brother in Christ. Paul strongly hints for Philemon to do even more, but he writes in allusive, metaphorical, and deliberately indirect ways, so that twenty-first-century readers must attempt to infer exactly what happened, what was happening, what exactly Paul meant to say in his remarks, and what the situation and the outcome were likely to have been.

Brogdon reads Paul's letter carefully and asks about the accuracy and adequacy of the traditional slave-flight construal of the letter. He frames matters of content and issues of interpretation clearly, so that his readers are well informed; and Brogdon's close exegetical work with the text of Paul's letter is both instructive and persuasive. Perhaps chief among Brogdon's incisive interpretive questions is this: How are we to understand Onesimus's *not* having been a Christian when he was at first in Philemon's household— but, that he became a Christian when separated from Philemon, and according to Paul, as he wrote the letter, some reconciliation was being sought. In turn, in this present study, Brogdon's reading of Paul's letter raises questions concerning the issues of privilege, social status, participation in community life, and radical acceptance; and in doing so, Brogdon presents a fresh, insightful, thought-provoking, and inspiring interpretation of Paul's letter to Philemon.

Paul's letter is a gem. It's a striking example of the greatly underappreciated wit and wisdom of the Apostle Paul. Brogdon's study identifies and brings into the bright light of new understanding many ways in which this little letter has so much to say. Brogdon teaches his readers to see and to appreciate Paul's often-unrecognized and profound theology, his subtle linguistic nuances, and his delightful, imaginative discussion of the situation that he is addressing. Certainly the matter addressed by Paul in this letter is serious, but at the same time the note of grace that can be heard throughout the whole composition keeps this important and thoughtful communication from sinking into sheer severe solemnity. Brogdon's own original insights concerning the disastrous practice of an exclusive fellowship (Brogdon's *Exclusionary Koinōnia*) in the life of the Christian community say a great deal to all who may desire to hear what Paul's first-century words have to communicate to twenty-first-century ears. Brogdon helps his readers perceive the depth and import of Paul's message in fresh and helpful ways. The serious and crucial nature of the topic of the letter to Philemon is never lost, although in his investigation and interpretation Brogdon gives the gem a good cleaning and puts it in a new setting for his and Paul's readers to see.

Marion L. Soards
Lousiville, Kentucky

Introduction

Is Philemon in the Bible?

THERE ARE TIMES I feel I am an anomaly in the church. I have had the distinct honor of writing my master's thesis and doctoral dissertation on the book of Philemon, a book in the Bible that I have come to realize many Christians do not recognize nor read. When I teach from the book of Philemon in a church, seminary, or university classroom the common response is bewilderment. I have grown accustomed to puzzled faces and even chuckle watching their expressions. Some people in church and class do not even know how to pronounce Philemon. I find the letter to Philemon to be one of the most interesting books in the Bible but I am not sure many others share this belief. Though the letter to Philemon was important enough to include in the canon of Scripture, it is often forgotten. For example, I grew up in the church and have spent my entire adult life in churches and can honestly say that I have never heard a sermon based on Philemon and have only heard one Bible study lesson on it. That is one lesson (besides the lessons I have taught) in the forty-four years I have been alive. And sadly, I am not alone. In my experience, Philemon is one of the books in the Bible that is often ignored and rarely read or studied by Christians.

Someone may respond, "Maybe that's unique to the churches and schools where you have taught." So I began sharing my work and interest in the letter to Philemon with the hundreds of pastors and church leaders I work with as an administrator and religious scholar. Over the past seven years, I have found that these colleagues rarely read and studied the letter themselves but were interested in learning more about my work. I wanted to test my experience on a few colleagues' congregations to see what I would find. While preparing to write this book, I conducted a brief survey to measure peoples' knowledge of the book of Philemon. I asked a group of pastors to administer a survey in their churches that asked the following questions: (1) Where in the Bible is the book of Philemon (Old or New Testament)? (2) Who wrote the book of Philemon? (3) Have you read the book of Philemon? (4) What is this book about? (5) Have you heard a sermon or attended a Bible study based on this book? If so, what were some of the things said about the book? (6) For ministers only: Have you ever preached a sermon or taught a Bible study lesson on Philemon and what were some of the things you preached/taught? I will focus on two churches from the Bible belt because they yielded some very interesting and revealing results.

I will begin with what I will call **Church A**. Regarding the question of the location of this letter in the Bible, seventy-five percent of participants in one congregation answered that the letter to Philemon was in the Old Testament. Fifty percent of participants did not know Paul was the author of the letter to Philemon and had not read the letter. Only twenty-five percent of participants understood any aspect of the letter's meaning and not a single person had heard a sermon or Bible study lesson on it. **Church**

B yielded better results. One hundred percent of the participants knew that the letter to Philemon was in the New Testament and ninety percent attributed the letter to Paul. Eighty percent of participants read the letter while sixty percent understood some aspect of its teaching. Last, similarly to **Church A**, ninety percent of participants in **Church B** had not heard a sermon or Bible study on Philemon. In fact, neither pastor had preached a sermon from Philemon, though one conducted a Bible study discussing forgiveness.

This was a small-scale survey conducted in a sample audience to generally gauge the knowledge of American church members. I understand that the findings are not comprehensive, but I believe the results, coupled with my years of work as a minister and biblical scholar, are still meaningful. With that said, I offer three preliminary findings. First, many people are not familiar with the letter to Philemon in a basic sense: knowing where it is in the Bible, who authored it, and what the letter is about. Second, the letter to Philemon is rarely read and understood in a meaningful way that influences faith. Some of the responses to the question of the letter's meaning were very basic and generic and reflected a lack of understanding. Third, Christian ministers are not preaching and teaching from this book and this reality almost guarantees parishioners will continue to ignore this book. My work with this letter has showed me that Philemon lies in canonical obscurity— unread, ignored, misunderstood, and rarely influencing churches as they discern how to give witness to the Gospel in the world.

A good beginning question is, "Why should anyone read the letter to Philemon?" I believe Philemon is one of the more interesting writings in the Bible. There is so much more to it than people think. For example, the letter shows the early church struggling to understand its witness in the world. Philemon is a unique account of the church's struggle to live in the world but not be of the world. As awkward and uncomfortable as it sounds, slaves were a part of the early church. Philemon details how the institution of slavery in the Greco-Roman world affected the early Christian churches and provides insight into how the church and, namely, the Apostle Paul, viewed and treated slaves. The letter to Philemon is not only interesting, it is messy. It deals with a situation in the life of the church that is, at best, awkward and potentially embarrassing. The letter was addressed to a Christian leader in the church who was both highly respected by Paul and a slave owner. It is not too much of a stretch to realize how problematic this is for modern Christians. It is even more awkward that Paul is not offering a firm rebuke of the institution of slavery. He is sending the slave back to his master. However, a closer reading of the letter will reveal that the letter does not represent an endorsement of slavery but rather wrestles with the effect of one's position "in Christ" on earthly relationships and social norms. Some commentators view the letter of Philemon as a severe critique against slavery because it introduced a new kind of relationship transcending old relationships while not necessarily changing the order of the world. When considering the challenges the church faces today, I hope to encourage more people to read and, more importantly, to study this small Pauline letter.

INTRODUCTION TO THE LETTER

The letter to Philemon is the eighteenth book in the New Testament located in a section containing four letters of Paul written to individuals (yes, Philemon is in the Bible). It was written by the Apostle Paul most likely between 61–63 CE from a prison in Rome (vv. 1, 9, 13) and was delivered to

Philemon by Tychicus and Onesimus (Col 4:9). Philemon was a pastor in the church at Colossae. Paul referred to him as a dear friend and fellow-worker (v. 1) and gave thanks to God because he heard of the faith and love that Philemon had for all the saints and prayed for Philemon to be active in the "sharing of faith" so he will have a fuller understanding of every good thing the church has in Jesus Christ (vv. 4–7). Instead of exerting apostolic authority on Philemon and ordering him to comply with his request, he appealed to Philemon in love (vv. 8–9). Paul wrote concerning Onesimus, a slave of Philemon, who, for reasons not explicitly stated in the letter, left his master's house and met up with Paul in Rome. Interestingly, Onesimus became a Christian through Paul's influence (v. 10). Together in prison, Paul found Onesimus to be very helpful and dear to him and his ministry (vv. 11–13, 16). In fact, Onesimus was so helpful that Paul wanted to keep him but would not use his influence as an apostle and keep him without Philemon's consent (vv. 13–14). Instead, he decided to send Onesimus back to Philemon because it is possible that there were deeper reasons for the separation between master and slave (vv. 12, 15). Because of this possibility, Paul instructed that Philemon welcome Onesimus back no longer as a slave but better than a slave, as a beloved brother in the flesh and in the Lord (vv. 16–17). He also promised that if Philemon was wronged he will repay him upon being released from prison (vv. 18, 19, 22). Paul concluded the letter by asking Philemon to refresh his heart, which was a potential veiled request to allow Onesimus to return to Paul and continue working with him. It is also possible that this request is for Philemon to manumit Onesimus (vv. 16, 20–22).

An additional important point worth mentioning is the public nature of the letter. The letter to Philemon was written not only to Philemon but also to the church that meets in his house (vv. 1–2). In the opening verses, Paul named Timothy as coauthor, greets Philemon, Apphia, Archippus, and the church that met in Philemon's house. Later in the letter, Paul informed Philemon that seven people who were with him (outside the household) were also aware of the situation: Tychicus, Aristarchus, Mark, Jesus (Justus), Epaphras, Luke, and Demas (Col 4:7–18; vv. 1, 23–24). This meant Paul knew that the letter would be read publicly to the church. Although the letter was addressed to Philemon, the situation that it addressed was not handled privately. At least eleven people were specifically named in addition to the church, which made it both public and exerted some degree of pressure and accountability on this church leader.

Now that I have made some general observations of the letter, I will begin to discuss its interpretation with three important preliminary observations. First, because of its brevity, the letter to Philemon does not provide enough detail to understand exactly what is going on between the people mentioned. This is the briefest Pauline letter, with only twenty-five verses consisting of 335 words in the Greek text, so there is not a lot to read. This means that exegetes must work with the available information in the letter, other Pauline writings like Colossians, and extra-biblical sources that provide information about the lives of slave masters and slaves in order to draw measured conclusions about possible events that prompted Paul to write the letter. Second, in one sense, Paul is being very careful in the letter, but in another sense, he seems to subtly encourage Philemon and this church to respond in a certain way. There are wordplays, subtle and overt comments about his wishes, and loaded statements—his meaning is open to interpretation but suggestive that he is weighing on the situation.

Wordplays	Subtle yet Overt Statements	Loaded/Bold Statements
Paul refers to himself as a "prisoner" in vv. 1, 13. There is a double meaning here. Paul is in prison in Rome and in a sense a prisoner of Christ Jesus, a prisoner to the work of the gospel, which is why he is imprisoned and suffers.	Paul tells Philemon that "in Christ" he could order him to do what is right in v. 8 but rather appeals to him in love as an old man and prisoner in v. 9.	Paul prays that Philemon's fellowship of faith may be effective through knowledge of the good in us by Christ in v. 6. This is a clear indication that he is a referring to the situation with Onesimus.
The name Onesimus means useful (v. 10). Paul tells Philemon that he wants some benefit from him in the Lord in v. 20. This is a veiled request for Onesimus to return to him.	Paul tells Philemon that he wished Onesimus could stay with him in v. 13 but did not want to force him to do this in v. 14.	Paul tells Philemon that he and Onesimus were separated for a time so he could have him back forever in a different manner before the writing of the letter in vv. 15–16.
The name Onesimus means useful (v. 10). Paul puns the meaning of his name in v. 11, telling Philemon that he once thought of him as useless but he is useful.	Paul gives thanks that Philemon refreshes the hearts of the saints in v. 7. He refers to Onesimus as his very heart in v. 12 and concludes by asking Philemon to refresh his heart in v. 20.	Paul tells Philemon that he should receive Onesimus back no longer as a slave but as a brother, a beloved brother, as a person and in the Lord in v. 16.
		Paul tells Philemon to receive Onesimus, a slave, the same as he would receive him, an apostle, in v. 17.

Wordplays	Subtle yet Overt Statements	Loaded/Bold Statements
		Paul reminds Philemon that he owes his very self to him in v. 19.
		Paul is confident that Philemon will obey his request and go beyond it in v. 21.
		Paul concludes by telling Philemon to prepare a guest room for him to visit after his release in v. 22.

Paul is addressing the situation in a delicate manner for a reason. Paul may be attempting to draw attention away from the fault of Onesimus to affect reconciliation with Philemon or not to further embarrass Onesimus for his flight. He may be writing this way not to shame Philemon for wrongdoing or even to protect Onesimus from further punishment by embarrassing Philemon in front of the church. Paul is careful throughout the letter but subtly assertive.

Third, there are some basic details about this letter that scholars generally agree on. Scholars generally agree on one of two dates for the letter and place of writing. The letter was written in the mid-fifties during an imprisonment in Ephesus or the early sixties while Paul was under arrest in Rome.[1] Scholars generally agree that Philemon

1. Fitzmyer, *Letter to Philemon*, 9–11; Barth and Blanke, *Epistle of Philemon*, 122–23. Scholars argue for two probable dates: 55–57 or 61–63. Fitzmyer dates the letter between 55–57 CE for the following reasons: historical precedent for it in the Marcionite prologue to the epistle to the Colossians; the connection of Philemon to the epistle to the Colossians, which is somewhat consistent with his lengthy

was a church leader of good report. We believe that Philemon became a Christian through Paul's influence and that he respects Paul. It is apparent that something happened between Philemon and Onesimus that resulted in the latter's departure. Onesimus journeys to Rome where Paul is under house arrest, and during his time there he becomes a Christian. We also believe that Paul became very fond of Onesimus, who was very helpful to him, and Paul most likely wanted to continue working with Onesimus but was legally obligated to send him back to his master. This basic storyline is widely accepted by scholars but there is much in the letter that is unclear and raises questions. The four most pressing questions are: (1) What is the exact nature of the relationship between Philemon and Onesimus?[2] (2) Why is Onesimus with Paul in prison? (3) Why is Onesimus converted to the faith in prison by Paul and not in the

ministry there circa 55–57; it has the advantage of keeping Philemon in Colossae and Paul in Ephesus within a plausible distance; and it more easily explains Paul's plan to visit in v 22. Barth and Blanke discussed those who argue for the 61–63 date. There are Greek manuscripts of Philemon that contain "written from Rome." Some contend that the epistle to the Colossians was written from Rome, which was a prominent place of refuge for slaves. Moreover, Roman imprisonment is consistent with Acts 28:16, in which Paul was kept in a relatively loose form of captivity. This author opts for the latter date, in spite of the problems with either date.

2. Knox, *Philemon*. John Knox offered a radically different picture of the master-slave relation. He argued that Paul was actually appealing to Archippus, who was the master of Onesimus, and therefore appeals to Philemon whose added weight as a church leader would ameliorate the situation. In the letter to the Colossians, Paul sends word to Archippus to "fulfill the ministry that you have received" (4:17), which for Knox means releasing Onesimus and allowing his return to Paul's side. Knox's thesis has some problems (what if Paul were imprisoned in Rome, v. 15b seems to imply that Paul expects Onesimus to stay), but nonetheless illustrates the debate over the exact nature of the relationship between Philemon and Onesimus.

household of Philemon? and (4) What is Paul asking Phile-mon to do about Onesimus?

In their respective ways, each question highlights the interpretive issues presented by the letter, specifically, what occurred between Onesimus and Philemon and how these events affect the interpretation of the letter. Again, these questions require interpreters to make a number of inferences about what led to the letter's writing and to con-struct a historical occasion or backstory that is utilized to interpret this brief text. I will begin with a thorough study of the dominant and traditional interpretation of the let-ter to Philemon and how it reconstructs the events that prompted Paul to put pen to paper. I begin here because this interpretation pervades the religious imagination of many Christians.

OVERVIEW OF THE BOOK

The first chapter is critically important because it lays out the reasons the church needs to take the interpretation of this letter in new directions already hinted at by a growing number of New Testament scholars. Before exploring new directions, I will spend considerable time challenging the standard interpretation of the letter to Philemon, which is the slave flight interpretation. Even though this interpreta-tion is still recognized as the best plausible way to under-stand the events that led Paul to pen this personal letter, it has serious exegetical, historical, cultural, and theological problems. I believe this standard interpretation is a root cause of the common neglect of Philemon by thoughtful Christians who are deeply commitment to justice.

Chapter two entitled, *Reimagining the Interpretation of Philemon*, explores the ways New Testament scholars have begun to take the interpretation of this text in new directions. I begin with the important work of Sarah Winter and Peter Lampe and move to focus on the contributions of four African American biblical scholars: Lloyd Lewis, Clarice Martin, Cain Felder, and Allen D. Callahan. These scholars were instrumental in re-centering the interpretation of Philemon. However, the most important part of the chapter is the exclusionary koinōnia interpretation. This interpretation is based on work I began in my doctoral dissertation. It is a new, constructive interpretation of the letter to Philemon that draws on the significant contributions of New Testament scholars and insights gleaned over a decade of studying this letter. The exclusionary koinōnia interpretation focuses on Onesimus and the historic belief that he was a major reason the letter was included in the canon in the first place. The focus on Onesimus is an interpretation that agrees with a prominent patristic father Ignatius.

The remaining two chapters are exegetical and theological in nature. Chapter three is an exegetical study of Philemon that shows Onesimus's exclusion in the house of Philemon was the central issue of the letter and was why Onesimus was not converted until leaving his house. Key sections such as the thanksgiving in vv. 4–7 and vv. 8, 11, and 16–17 are examined in a new light, illuminating our understanding of this important text and providing a much better foundation to engage the church theologically, which is the focus of the final chapter where I launch out into deeper theological waters. In this chapter I demonstrate how the exclusionary koinōnia interpretation can better serve the church because it asks questions such as, "What happens when the church does not go far enough in its commitment to the gospel?" and addresses issues such as how exclusion and injustice impede salvation, koinōnia as the deepening of faith, the role of advocacy in reconciliation, and how modern-day Onesimuses can lead to the revitalization of the church. There is so much theological material in this letter once it is reinterpreted that touches on issues the church is struggling with today. That is why I believe Philemon is a letter the church cannot afford to ignore. In the end, the exclusionary koinōnia interpretation of Philemon provides a way to both assess this text's problematic history while finding ways to interpret it in more redemptive and liberating ways.

Chapter 1

Challenging the Slave Flight Interpretation of Philemon

AN IMPORTANT FIRST STEP in offering a new interpretation of this New Testament text is to examine the dominant and prevailing interpretation and attempt to illumine its limitations and problems. It is only after this that one can see the need to reimagine this letter's message. The slave flight interpretation is the dominant theory of the letter's historical occasion and has been utilized by prominent figures in the Christian tradition, such as John Chrysostom, Jerome, Ambrosiaster, Theodore of Mopsuesta, and Thomas Aquinas. Reformation figures, such as Martin Luther and John Calvin, also held to the slave flight hypothesis. This interpretation has dominated the church since the fourth century. Most New Testament introductions, as well as English, French, German, and even African commentaries, use the slave flight hypothesis as the basis of their interpretations.

The slave flight hypothesis is an interpretation of the letter to Philemon arguing the following: Philemon was a Christian leader and likely an owner of slaves and one of his slaves was named Onesimus. Onesimus was not a good slave. Scholars suggest that he was a useless and unprofitable slave (v. 11) who wronged Philemon, most likely by robbing his master (v. 18) and fleeing his house (v. 15a). Afterwards, Onesimus found his way to Paul who was in prison in Rome, became a Christian (v. 10), and proved to be very useful to Paul (vv. 11–12), who sent the slave back to his master. In the letter, Paul requests that Philemon forgive Onesimus instead of punishing him and accept him as a brother in the Lord now that he was a believer (v. 16). He even promises to repay Philemon for whatever Onesimus took from Philemon (v. 18), and he was confident that Philemon would heed Paul's request (vv. 16, 21). He promised to visit the church after his release and follow up on the matter (v. 22).

There are many scholars who believe this story line makes the most sense, mainly because it fits the common narrative of runaway slaves seeking freedom. Scholars such as John G. Nordling argue that there is evidence in the ancient world of "uniform pattern of runaway slave behavior, which Onesimus may well have adopted before he met Paul and departed from his former manner of life."[1] Nordling and many other scholars often refer to a letter from Pliny the Younger to Sabinianus. In this letter, Pliny tried to reconcile a runaway slave with his master.

> Your freedman, whom you had mentioned as having displeased you, has come to me; he threw himself at my feet and clung to them as he could have to yours. He cried much, begged constantly, even with much silence; in short, he has convinced me that he repents of what he did. I truly believe that he is reformed, because he recognizes that he has been delinquent. You are

1. Nordling, "Onesmimus Fugitivus," 99.

angry, I know, and rightly so, as I also recognize; but clemency wins the highest praise when the reason for anger is most righteous. You once had affection for (this) human being, and, I hope, you will have it again. Meanwhile it suffices that you let me prevail upon you. Should he again incur your displeasure, you will have so much more reason to be angry, as you give in now. Allow somewhat for his youth, for his tears, and for your own indulgent conduct. Do not antagonize him, lest you antagonize yourself at the same time; for when a man of your mildness is angry, you will be antagonizing yourself. I fear that, in joining my entreaties to his, I may seem rather to compel than to request (you to forgive him). Nevertheless, I shall join them so much more fully and unreservedly, because I have sharply and severely reproved him, positively threatening never to entreat again on his behalf. Although I said this to him, who should become more fearful (of offending), I do not say it to you. I may perhaps have occasion to entreat you again and obtain your forgiveness, but may it be such that it will be proper for me to intercede and you to pardon. Farewell.[2]

Pliny's letter resembles the situation of the letter to Philemon. It provides a historical point of contact between the situation in Philemon's house to situations others faced with slaves. Using Pliny's letter to interpret Paul's letter provides viable answers to issues like the exact nature of the relationship between Philemon and Onesimus and the reason for Onesimus's departure. If the two letters are seen as parallel, this would mean that Paul, like Pliny, was writing the letter to smooth things over with Philemon, now that Onesimus has changed his ways. Paul not only wanted Philemon to

2. Younger, *Epistles*, 9:21.

forgive his wayward slave but also to do something radical that reflected the depth of Christian bonds. Paul wanted Philemon to accept him back, no longer as a slave but as a brother, and he promised to pay for the damage caused by Onesimus's theft.

This interpretation provides answers for three of the four pressing questions: (1) What was the exact nature of the relationship between Philemon and Onesimus? (2) Why was Onesimus with Paul, who was in prison? (3) Why was Onesimus converted to the faith in prison by Paul and not in the household of Philemon? and (4) What was Paul asking Philemon to do about Onesimus? This standard interpretation maintains that Philemon was the master of his slave Onesimus, who was in prison with Paul because he fled the house of his master. It also asserts that Paul was asking Philemon to forgive his slave's theft and flight and also was asking Philemon to receive his slave back as a brother in the flesh and in the Lord. However, this interpretation does not address the issue of Onesimus's conversion outside of the house of Philemon. The slave flight hypothesis offers a compelling backstory that fits the first century practice of some slaves running away from their masters, but there are some gaps and problems with this hypothesis. Slave flight interpretation has a web of exegetical, historical, cultural, and theological problems that should cause both scholars and Christian readers to reevaluate its use for the church today.

EXEGETICAL PROBLEMS WITH THE SLAVE FLIGHT INTERPRETATION

The first exegetical problem with this interpretation is inferred. Paul did not state that Onesimus ran away from the house of Philemon in any of the twenty-five verses of this letter. Why do scholars and interpreters believe Onesimus ran away? They make three arguments to defend the slave flight hypothesis. First, some interpret the phrase "he was separated" in v. 15 as a euphemism for flight.[3] Second, when scholars account for the absence of any reference to flight in the letter, they reason that Paul intended to divert attention from the fault of the slave.[4] In this case, the failure to refer to any fault improved Paul's chances of effecting forgiveness and reconciliation. Third, scholars turn to Greco-Roman culture and argue that slaves often ran away from masters. For example, John Nordling examined extrabiblical texts that mention runaway slaves and Roman law, which gave precedent and context for what was allegedly being reported in the letter. In varying ways, these arguments were deployed to support the slave flight hypothesis. While the flight of Onesimus provides a story that makes some sense of statements in Philemon, it is a stretch to conclude Onesimus robbed his master and ran away based on statements made by Paul in vv. 10–18. As Callahan rightly comments, there are no verbs for flight in the letter, no rationale offered for his flight, nor motive for his flight in the letter.[5] Scholars have inferred flight based on evidence outside the letter itself and understandings of the behavior of slaves that are more cultural than exegetical.

There is a second exegetical problem with the slave flight interpretation. It is clear that Paul is being careful in the letter, but neither the reason for this nor the inference of flight are convincing. For example, in the following two lengthy quotes, John Barclay and John Nordling offer their explanations for Paul's care in how he wrote to Philemon.

---

3. Nordling, "Onesmimus Fugitivus," 109.

4. Barclay, "Paul, Philemon, and the Dilemma," 164.

5. Callahan, "Paul's Epistle to Philemon," 357–58.

There seem to be good reasons for holding to the usual understanding of events. The fact that the letter makes no explicit reference to Onesimus running away is not conclusive evidence that he did not do so. A tactful letter of appeal written on behalf of a runaway might well avoid referring directly to the offending facts, and in this light it is easy to see why Paul should use the vague expression . . . in v. 15, especially as the passive carries possible connotations of the divine will. Indeed, the extraordinarily tactful approach that Paul adopts throughout this letter is a clear indication that he recognizes that he is dealing with a delicate situation in which Philemon could well react awkwardly. . . . It is almost inconceivable that Paul should mention such negative details concerning his protégé unless they were a major obstacle in the relationship between Philemon and Onesimus.[6]

Paul's purposes in writing to Philemon prevented him from describing Onesimus in the usual terms. The runaway slave hypothesis seems quite plausible if Paul described Onesimus's past crimes against his master in an oblique and euphemistic manner. Even if Paul were fully aware of the runaway slave racket and of the financial loss Philemon suffered as a result of Onesimus's flight, we should not expect him to badger Philemon with painful reminders of details already known too well. Paul's purpose here is primarily conciliatory: to persuade Onesimus's angry owner to welcome back his previously disobedient slave: προσλαβοῦ αὐτὸν ὡς ἐμέ ["Receive him as me"] (v. 17b). To accomplish this Paul strives to present Onesimus in the best possible

6. Barclay, "Paul, Philemon, and the Dilemma," 164.

> light, recalls Philemon's past services to Paul and
> other saints (vv. 5, 7), and even engages in a mild
> form of flattery . . . to induce Philemon to com-
> ply with the apostle's radical request.[7]

For Barclay and Nordling, Paul was being tactful because Philemon was upset. He was offended and dishonored. His slave, who was believed to be useless, had wronged
him and in an indirect way had embarrassed Philemon in
front of the church. Paul wanted to take attention away
from this and focus on reconciling master and slave. So his
careful and euphemistic language, as well as compliments
given about Philemon and Onesimus, reflected attempts
to assuage Philemon's anger and encourage him to forgive.
However, this reason does not really make sense. Why does
Paul need to be careful or "tactful" if flight was common
among slaves? Nordling and others spend a great amount
of time building a case for the widespread practice of slave
flight, a practice he documents from the first to fourth
century CE. For slave flight interpreters, slaves offended
their masters by not doing their assigned tasks, stealing,
and running away. That is what slaves do. If that's the case,
there really is no reason to tip-toe around such a common
issue with euphemisms and loaded statements. Philemon
would have no reason to be embarrassed by the flight of
a "useless" slave who robbed him and was being returned.
Furthermore, with Onesimus's recent conversion, which
entailed the confession of his sins in some way, why would
Onesimus have had a problem acknowledging his fault in
the matter? There really was no reason for Paul to protect
Onesimus from embarrassment, if he caused it. After all,
this would have been a helpful first step in his understanding of contrition, repentance, and community, all ideas Paul
taught the church at Corinth (2 Cor 2:5–11; 7:2–16).

7. Nordling, "Onesmimus Fugitivus," 107.

Paul's careful use of language may have reflected a central issue that the slave flight hypothesis does not even address, which is the conversion of Onesimus outside of Philemon's house. There may be reasons Onesimus was not a Christian in Philemon's house and these reasons may be related to his departure and stay with Paul. Onesimus may not have been a Christian because of the poor example of the Christian faith he observed in Philemon, who welcomed others but mistreated and excluded him, a slave. I suspect that Paul was being careful and shrewd because Philemon has some fault in this. Onesimus was in a vulnerable position delivering this letter, because if he embarrassed or humiliated Philemon in front of the church, he would suffer for it, not Paul.

There are other exegetically related problems with this interpretation of Philemon among scholars who still use it. Douglas Moo's careful work on Philemon in the Pillar New Testament Series is one example of this. He is an advocate of the slave flight hypothesis in spite of the lack of any actual reference to flight in the letter. I include this because it provides further evidence of the abundance of problems one encounters trying to defend this interpretation exegetically. He identifies three problems one encounters when defending the belief in Onesimus's flight. First, if Onesimus was indeed a runaway slave, then he had legally "wronged" Philemon. Yet Paul discussed Onesimus's wrongdoing of Philemon only as a possibility (v. 18). Second, and related to the first point, we would have expected a runaway slave returning to his master for reconciliation to express remorse. Yet, Paul never discussed Onesimus's repentance or remorse in the letter. The third and most serious objection to the runaway slave view is the difficulty imagining how Paul and Onesimus ever would have met one another.[8]

8. Moo, *Letters to the Colossians*, 367.

A slave running away and coincidentally meeting up with Paul in prison, rather than hiding, does not make much sense. These issues notwithstanding, Moo leans slightly in favor of the slave flight hypothesis and focuses on v. 17, "Welcome him [Onesimus] as you would welcome me." In other words, the central issue of the letter is Paul's request for Philemon to welcome a slave as a brother in Christ, a common theme found in Philemon studies.[9] We almost automatically think it is about a runaway slave, the dominate narrative we heard in Sunday school and learned in seminary. Paul, knowing the law regarding runaway slaves, wrote a letter to the master Philemon to accept his runaway slave back as a Christian brother. We then think of this letter as modeling Christian practices such as forgiveness, reconciliation, and familial bonds that Christians share (we are all brothers and sisters in Christ regardless of social location). Is the letter to Philemon really about forgiveness and reconciliation or even that Christians are sisters and brothers? This question underscores my concerns with this interpretation, which are deeper theological problems.

HISTORICAL PROBLEMS WITH THE SLAVE FLIGHT INTERPRETATION

The second set of problems is historical in nature. This interpretation of Philemon has a deeply problematic history that most New Testament scholars avoid or ignore altogether, as if one can divorce exegesis from history. A study of the history of the interpretation of Philemon will show that major Christian interpreters used this letter and the slave flight interpretation to implicitly support slavery by arguing that Christianity makes slaves better fit to serve their masters. And the implicit "proslavery" hermeneutic

9. Ibid., 369–70.

that undergirds the slave flight interpretation paved the way for the church in later periods to defend slavery explicitly.

The implicit "proslavery" hermeneutic began with John Chrysostom, the fifth century bishop of Antioch. In many respects, his commentary on Philemon became the standard for many others in the church. He valued this letter because Paul showed concern for Onesimus, whom he referred to as "a runaway, a thief, and a robber."[10] He asserted that the letter directed the church not to abandon slaves, even if they were wicked. More importantly, he insisted that Paul's actions in the letter seemed to instruct the church not to remove slaves from their masters.[11] What is even more revealing are his comments on v. 16 in which he concluded that by becoming a Christian, Onesimus would become a "more honorable slave," one that is "more well-disposed than a brother," and one that "will not run away."[12] The image of the gospel making a "well disposed" slave who would not run away was striking and sadly paradigmatic for later interpreters.

Others followed Chrysostom, including the medieval Catholic theologian, Thomas Aquinas. He also used the slave flight hypothesis to interpret this letter. Through that lens, he taught on the master-slave relationship in the prologue of his commentary on Philemon. First, he quoted Eccl 33:31 that states, "If thou have a faithful servant, let him be to thee as thy own soul; treat him as a brother." This verse was important to him because it disclosed what was required for slaves, what ought to have been the feeling of masters toward slaves, and how masters should have used slaves. For Aquinas, slaves should be faithful and masters

10. Chrysostom, "Homilies," in Schaff, *Nicene and Post-Nicene Fathers*, 546.

11. Ibid.

12. Ibid., 552.

should be friendly, treating slaves as brothers. Second, similar to Chrysostom's interpretive reasoning, Aquinas contended that the letter "shows how temporal masters ought to relate to their temporal slaves and how the faithful servant ought to relate to his master."[13]

Martin Luther and John Calvin, to varying degrees, illustrated this same interpretive tendency in their respective commentaries on Philemon. For Luther, the book of Philemon expounds upon the doctrines of Christ as it relates to the situation between Philemon and Onesimus. It also demonstrates how to handle a breach of the faith. Regarding v. 10, on the conversion of Onesimus, Luther explained that his new condition as a Christian would not lead to his release. He argued, rather, that Paul "indeed confirms his servitude."[14] Onesimus was at that point both a slave of Philemon and a son of Paul. Luther concluded from v. 12 that Paul sent Onesimus back, not asking for freedom, but to return to a more effective servitude. He also interpreted v. 16 to mean that Onesimus would "serve with spontaneous obedience" and steadfast service. Luther believed the gospel taught "that this ought to be done."[15] Luther's interpretation of Philemon was clearly sympathetic to slavery.

Paul's letter to Philemon was valuable to Calvin because the apostle condescended or demeaned himself to address both a subject that he considered "low and mean" and to address a "man of lowest condition."[16] He marveled that an apostle condescended to take up the matter of a slave. Calvin reinforced this theme again in v. 10, noting how deeply Paul condescended to elevate Onesimus, calling a runaway slave and thief "son." Furthermore, he asserted

13. Aquinas, *Commentaries*, 197.

14. Luther, *Works of Martin Luther*, 103.

15. Ibid.

16. Calvin, *Epistles*, 347.

that Onesimus's flight was a benefit because of his conversion, and also that he would thus become a "useful slave and brother."[17] There was nothing in Philemon that Calvin drew on to challenge slavery. What stood out for him was Paul addressing the issue in the first place. Calvin's underlying assumption that slaves are socially inferior was the lens through which he interpreted Paul's condescension.

The slave flight hypothesis, with centuries of theological development, influenced chattel slavery in the United States and served a major role in the explicit defense of slavery from the Bible. Millions of Africans were enslaved in the Americas. The sanction of the church and the interpretation of the Bible were all sad parts of this history. The slave flight interpretation of Philemon was instrumental in the nineteenth century debates over the biblical sanction for slavery and the defense of the Fugitive Slave Act of 1850 in the antebellum era. In his book *Slaveholding Not Sinful*, written in 1855, Samuel B. How argued that Philemon, though a slaveholder, was commended for his love and faith. In particular, How asserted that Paul's response in this letter established a "precedent to guide the church in all future similar cases."[18] The precedent that Paul appears to have established was Philemon's full and explicit right to have slaves and to have fugitive slaves returned. In a similar manner, George Junkin interpreted Philemon as proof of God's acceptance of slavery. In fact, he ardently contended "that there is not a sentence in the New Testament which gives ground for the logical inference that the simple holding of a slave, or slaves, was inconsistent with Christian profession and Christian character."[19] Another example of interpreting Philemon in this vein comes from a

17. Ibid., 357.

18. How, *Slaveholding Not Sinful*, 26–27.

19. Junkin, "Proposition," in Priest, *Bible Defense of Slavery*, 625.

Presbyterian minister, George Armstrong. In his proslavery tract written in 1857, *The Christian Doctrine of Slavery*, he used the letter of Philemon as proof of God's approval of slavery since Paul sent a fugitive slave back to his Christian master after the slave's conversion. He understood this act to signify the master's right to the services of his slave.[20] This is a very problematic history.

The Fugitive Slave Act was passed in Congress on September 18, 1850, and it declared that all runaway slaves be brought back to their masters. The law forced authorities in northern states to return slaves to their owners in southern states. This law sparked a debate between abolitionists and apologists of slavery, and the church in America was divided on this issue. For example, Luther Lee, a Methodist pastor in New York, criticized the law and refused to obey it on the grounds that it was unjust, whereas Moses Stuart, a Baptist minister and professor at Andover Theological Seminary, defended the law on moral and legal grounds.[21] For ministers like Stuart and others who defended the Fugitive Slave Act, the letter to Philemon and the slave flight hypothesis was particularly helpful. It established the government's precedent to return slaves to their masters. They used this interpretation of Philemon to support the capture and return of enslaved Africans from the north to the south.[22] US Marshals and other slave catchers with dogs hunted enslaved Africans who sought freedom and returned them to bondage.

This interpretation was also used to indoctrinate enslaved Africans, pushing them to accept slavery as God's will and to commit themselves to being good slaves. In

20. Armstrong, *Christian Doctrine of Slavery*, 33.

21. See Stuart, *Conscience and Constitution*; and Thompson, *Fugitive Slave Law*.

22. Thompson, *Fugitive Slave Law*.

1833, Charles Colcock Jones, a white Presbyterian minister, was commissioned to preach to enslaved Africans, and he testified how his interpretation of Philemon was received. He stated,

> I was preaching to a large congregation on the Epistle to Philemon and when I insisted upon fidelity and obedience as Christian virtues in servants and upon the authority of Paul, condemned the practice of running away, one half of my audience deliberately rose up and walked off with themselves and those that remained looked anything but satisfied either with the preacher or his doctrine. After dismissal, there was no small stir among them; some solemnly declared that "there was no such epistle in the Bible," others, "that they did not care if they ever heard me preach again!"[23]

This incident shows the enslaved Africans' dissatisfaction with the proslavery interpretation of Philemon.

There is no escaping the fact that this history is linked to the slave flight interpretation. For over a century, Christian interpreters failed to challenge the practice of slavery and to apply a different and more liberating hermeneutic. In some instances, interpreters explicitly endorsed the continuation of this practice, and some even argued that Christianity makes better slaves. For over a century, the letter's theological value was inextricably linked to the practice of Christianized slavery, especially the explicit proslavery interpretations of Philemon during the antebellum era. The worst part of this history is the link between the slave flight interpretation and the suffering of enslaved Africans in America. These given reasons make this interpretation extremely problematic for the church to use today.

23. Raboteau, *Slave Religion*, 294–95.

CULTURAL PROBLEMS WITH THE SLAVE FLIGHT INTERPRETATION

The third set of problems with the slave flight interpretation is cultural. The slave flight argument not only has a problematic history, but it is also culturally offensive. Only a few scholars have picked up on the problematic assumptions undergirding this interpretation. For example, John Knox rightly characterizes it as a stereotype.[24] Barth and Blanke's commentary on Philemon also questioned whether there are prejudices against Onesimus.

> Ancient and later, including modern commentators on PHM, also monographs on Pauline ethics, appear to have a tacit understanding: it is the slave who had been guilty, not the master. . . . The common prejudice against the slave is not supported by solid evidence drawn from PHM; rather it may be the result of a bias on the side of interpreters. . . . PHM was almost exclusively expounded by men who were scholarly monks, priests, or pastors, established church leaders or academic lights, living in relatively safe positions, with better or worse domestics at hand. With very few exceptions, professional theologians are among the last to shed class prejudices.[25]

They have identified a much deeper problem that goes beyond the text. It challenges the assumptions interpreters bring to the text and exposes the influence of social location on interpretation. The letter to Philemon has been a victim of an entire class of interpreters who are biased and prejudiced.

---

24. Knox, *Philemon*, 10.
25. Barth and Blanke, *Letter*, 226–27.

Allen D. Callahan has provided the most insight into this aspect of the slave flight interpretation. He claims that the slave flight hypothesis "buys into the stereotype of the thieving, indolent slave which is a part of all slave-holding societies."[26] Callahan provides an assessment of what he believes is actually influencing interpreters in a response to the New Testament scholar Margaret Mitchell after her critique of his interpretation that Philemon and Onesimus were estranged brothers. He says,

> [T]he fugitive slave hypothesis put forward by Chrysostom and others reflects the interests of a class of interpreters as opposed to a historically defensible reconstruction of the original *Sitz im Leben* of the letter. . . . The traditional interpretation of Philemon is still eisegetical, and has been propped up with a reconstructed narrative that, as I have shown, is saturated with the kind of hostile stereotypes of the slave purveyed by the master class in all slave regimes. The degree to which John Chrysostom or any other commentator accepted this aspect of master class ideology is an important issue, but is necessarily secondary to the recognition of the ideology itself and the interests it serves.[27]

Callahan uncovers deeper cultural problems with this interpretation in the plethora of unjustified inferences and prejudices about slaves, which were imposed on the historical occasion by mostly white scholars.[28] These scholars began with the belief that since flight was a common practice among slaves in the Greco-Roman world, Onesimus, the slave, must have been doing the same. That assumption has

26. Callahan, *Embassy*, 361.

27. Callahan, "John Chrysostom," 149–50.

28. Ibid.

a cultural component to it, because for Callahan, "nowhere does the epistle explicitly state that Onesimus has run away, and the motive for the action is equally obscure."[29] In their attempt to identify the one guilty of wrongdoing, scholars who hold to the slave flight hypothesis assume that the malefactor must have been Onesimus. Foundational to this assumption lies the historic or traditional argument that Onesimus was a slave and worse yet, a pilfering slave.

Nowhere are biases and prejudices more evident than in how scholars study and view slavery. I find many to be sympathetic to owning slaves. In the provocative text, *Slavery as Salvation*, Dale Martin contends that despite recent advances in knowledge regarding Greco-Roman slavery by classicists and historians, biblical scholars often present a monolithic picture of slavery. One reason for this picture of slavery has been the biblical scholar's privileged choice of sources. These scholars look to the high literature of Greco-Roman culture and therefore tend to view slavery and slaves in a manner similar to the social elites of the Greco-Roman world, who were responsible for most of the written record from that era.[30] Martin's reference to a monolithic picture of slavery is important because it reinforces my point about the allegiance of scholars to the master class. They assume that if any wrong is done it was the fault of the slave, and so they bring that assumption to both their study of slavery in the ancient world and to the letter of Philemon.

Cultural bias runs even deeper than the historical occasion. It influences how exegetes view Philemon and Onesimus. I realized this when I compared references to Philemon and Onesimus made by Paul to comments made about Philemon and Onesimus by interpreters. This comparative study highlighted the tendency to reflect master

29. Callahan, "Paul's Epistle to Philemon," 358.

30. Martin, *Slavery as Salvation*, xviii.

class interests and to use stereotypes about enslaved persons. I will begin by presenting first what is said of these two figures in the letter, and then examine how interpreters elaborate on these references in ways that reveal their cultural biases and level of comfort with the master.

Paul's description of Philemon in the letter can be drawn from a few key verses. He describes Philemon as a beloved fellow worker and a man with love and faith toward Jesus and all the saints (vv. 1, 5). He was also known for "refreshing the hearts of the saints," and his reputation was such that Paul was confident of Philemon's compliance with his request (vv. 7, 21). Chrysostom described Philemon as a man of "admirable and noble character," as evidenced by his Christian household and the fact that his house served as a lodging for saints.[31] Even Aquinas claimed that he was a "noteworthy Christian."[32] Martin Luther referred to Philemon as a bishop and "leader in the word."[33] In Luther's day, the title of bishop carried a different understanding than a bishop in the ancient world. In the church of Luther's day, the title bishop was a hierarchical designation that added even more weight to this claim. Calvin asserted that "Philemon belonged to the order of pastors" and later in v. 5, Paul "bestows on (him) . . . the whole perfection of a Christian man."[34] Antebellum proslavery exegetes reveled in the fact that Philemon, "though a slaveholder," was commended for his love and faith.[35] Prominent figures in the proslavery movement generally concluded from Paul's short letter that Philemon was a good Christian master to his slaves. In his

31. Chrysostom, "Homilies," in Schaff, *Nicene and Post-Nicene Fathers*, 545.

32. Aquinas, *Commentaries*, 198.

33. Luther, *Works of Martin Luther*, 94.

34. Calvin, *Commentaries*, 348–49.

35. How, *Slaveholding Not Sinful*, 26–27.

commentary published in 1875, J. B. Lightfoot character-ized Philemon as one who "proved worthy of his spiritual heritage," and further, that the title "fellow worker" in v. 1 "is a noble testimony to his evangelical zeal."[36] Contempo-rary descriptions of Philemon resemble those previously mentioned. Interpreters hold a flattering and overwhelm-ingly positive estimation of Philemon.[37] These inferences about Philemon exceed the evidence in the text.

Paul's description of Onesimus, drawn from vv. 10–13, 15–16, and 18, was equally complimentary. Onesimus was affectionately referred to as the child begotten of the apostle, as the apostle's heart, as one useful and desired for the work of ministry. Paul even alluded to God's providential work in the separation by writing that upon his return Onesimus would be received as beloved brother and no longer as a slave. But despite those favorable references to Onesimus in the epistle, the dominant orientation and prejudice toward Philemon as a benevolent slave master was situated against the backdrop of the constant demonization of Onesimus as a slave. Despite Paul's positive characterization of Onesi-mus, scholars used uncomplimentary and, at times, pejora-tive descriptions of him.

Among the church fathers, Chrysostom called him "a runaway, a thief, and a robber."[38] Thomas Aquinas added that, upon stealing, Onesimus secretly fled to Rome. With-in the Reformation period, Calvin followed this trajectory by calling Onesimus a "runaway slave and thief . . . a man of the lowest condition."[39] Worse yet, nineteenth century

36. Lightfoot, *Colossians and Philemon*, 130.

37. Barth and Blanke, *Letter*, 138; Fitzmyer, *Letter to Philemon*, 13.

38. Chrysostom, "Homilies," in Schaff, *Nicene and Post-Nicene Fathers*, 546.

39. Calvin, *Epistles of Paul*, 347–48.

characterizations degraded Onesimus, and slaves in general, ascribing to them the tendency for stealing and flight. One notable example comes not from a southern proslavery theologian, but a prominent scholar, J. B. Lightfoot:

> Onesimus represented the least respectable class in the social scale. He was regarded by philosophers as live chattel, a living implement. . . . He was now also a thief and a runaway. Rome was the natural cesspool for these offscourings of humanity. In the dregs of the city rabble was his best hope for secrecy. . . . This is none other than Onesimus whom Philemon will only remember as a worthless creature, altogether untrue to his name, but who now is a reformed man.[40]

His language clearly reflected class bias because these characterizations were not based on textual references to Philemon and Onesimus. Culture is a determining influence in interpretation. The treatments of Philemon as master and Onesimus as slave support this influence and betray the naiveté of interpreters who believe they are allowing the text to speak for itself. Referring to Philemon as a perfect Christian man or a bishop, while portraying Onesimus as a pilfering slave or worse yet a worthless creature, reveal influences outside of the text that were shaping the interpretative process. This is just one of the problematic ways scholars can align themselves with the master class and hold stereotypical beliefs about slaves.

One of the principal aims of anyone working in the field of African-American biblical interpretation is to challenge Eurocentrism by exposing the assumptions and underlying beliefs Euro-scholars impose on the text. Some white scholars impose their cultural perspectives and values onto the text of Scripture and assume their cultural vantage

40. Lightfoot, *Colossians and Philemon*, 131–33.

point is universal and normative for everyone. Scholars in African-American hermeneutics show that Eurocentric interpretations reflect their own cultural context and ignore the effect of these interpretations on minority cultures and scholars. Because the European context is the dominant interpretative influence on reading Philemon, this cultural lens has transmitted perspectives that are culturally incompatible for an African American and others reading from the margins.[41] The slave flight hypothesis utilizes master-slave ideology in inappropriate and deeply problematic ways. For this reason, Mitzi J. Smith argues, "African Americans must equally reject a master-slave mentality toward traditional scholarship that ignores the oppressive existential impact of such texts and repressive hermeneutics extracted from these texts."[42] Not only must African Americans reject the master-slave ideology undergirding the slave flight hypothesis, all scholars need to do so. But to do this, careful attention must be given to the pervasive influence of master-slave ideology undergirding the slave flight reading of Philemon.

THEOLOGICAL PROBLEMS WITH THE SLAVE FLIGHT INTERPRETATION

The fourth and greatest exegetical set of problems with the slave flight interpretation is theological. The slave flight interpretation severely limits the theological horizons of this text and results in a troubling tendency among interpreters in Christianizing slavery and slaveholding. Careful exegesis and the interpretation of Scripture are foundational to Christian theology. The kind of exegesis and interpretation

41. Smith, "Slavery in the Early Church," in Blount et al., *True to Our Native Land*, 18.

42. Ibid.

that undergirds the slave flight interpretation poses significant theological challenges for the church, especially in light of associated historical and cultural problems. There are two real problems with theology based on the slave flight hypothesis. First, scholars draw very little from the theological well of this letter. Marion Soards's study on the theological dimensions of the letter brought attention to the limited ways the letter can be used. He writes, "Few ideas in New Testament studies produce higher levels of agreement than the notion that Paul's letter to Philemon has little or no theological substance."[43] He chronicles a sixteen-hundred-year history of theological neglect that goes back to John Chrysostom, Theodore of Mopsuestia, and Jerome, and to modern scholars like John Knox and Norman Peterson. What Soards found is interesting. The letter to Philemon was read and studied for moral lessons that could be drawn from it and not for its theological teachings. In addition, he provides an insightful survey of theological statements in the letter. While Soards does not explore reasons for this pervasive belief about the letter to Philemon, I believe part of the neglect is the slave flight interpretation. It is both theologically limiting and problematic, which is the deeper and more pervasive problem with this way of interpretating.

The second problem with the slave flight interpretation is the refusal to problematize the master-slave relationship in any manner. This decision leaves scholars doing what I call "slave-master" theology. Slave-master theology is the kind of theology that uses stereotypes of enslaved and marginalized peoples, aligns itself with the master class, and tries to Christianize enslavement and other forms of oppression. Post-colonial, liberation, feminist, and womanist theologies all find such moves to be very problematic and, in many respects, wrong. Because of this recognition,

43. Soards, "Some Neglected Theological Dimensions," 209.

some scholars have begun to challenge the underlying beliefs and assumptions upon which the slave flight hypothesis rests, especially its historical and social implications for
marginalized groups.[44]

Feminist scholar Sabine Bieberstein's important work
on this subject maintains that "history is no longer related
as the story of the rulers, but is told anew as the story of the
victims."[45] She believes there should be a perspective shift
in the interpretation of texts like Philemon. In her essay, the
primary issue is the recognition of the victim, which is why
she views Onesimus as the victim within a larger system
of oppression. This perspective challenges and changes the
interpretive orientation of the letter, shifting the focus from
a preoccupation with the master to the difficult realities of
the slave. Her essay further exposes the deeper problem
with the slave flight hypothesis, its link to systemic oppression, and a long history of guilt.[46] Bieberstein's work shows
that the theological legacy of this interpretation is not only
limiting, it is unsound. Historically, Christian interpreters of Philemon were clearly on the side of the master and
sought both to sterilize and Christianize slavery. Culturally, slave stereotypes provided justification for centuries
of western colonialism and slavery. They also provided
theological ammunition for Christian masters in America
to use against enslaved Africans.

The theological problem begins with the tendency of
some scholars to Christianize slavery and by Christianizing
slavery they implicitly legitimize it. Scholars tend to make
two arguments, both providing a complimentary portrait

44. Lyons, "Paul's Confrontation with Class," 116–32; Bieberstein,
"Disrupting the Normal," 105–16; Callahan, "Paul's Epistle to Philemon," 357–76.

45. Bieberstein, "Disrupting the Normal," 114.

46. Ibid.

of slavery. First, they argue that ancient slavery was different than modern slavery, and, in some respects, that it was not as bad as modern slavery. Second, they argue Christian faith improves master-slave relations. Some scholars go to great lengths to argue there is marked difference between slavery in ancient world and modern times. One of the implicit, if not explicit, assumptions in the study of New Testament slavery is that modern forms of slavery and modern understandings of slavery should not be used in interpretation. Raymond Brown's New Testament introduction states, "The slavery many English speaking readers of the Bible are most familiar with is that of the blacks in America, but the Roman situation was more complicated."[47] In a more recent critical commentary, R. Wilson charges, "Our modern attitude is inevitably coloured by recollection of the slave trade, the transportation of black slaves from Africa to America to labour in the plantations." He even adds that ancient slavery is not entirely comparable, and, as a result, we should not "transpose our legitimate condemnation of the trade to the Americas back into ancient world, where the factors which forced people into slavery could have been entirely different."[48] Scholars argue that any interpretation of Philemon should not draw on African enslavement in America.

Even though scholars are correct in insisting there were differences between Greco-Roman and American slavery, they overstate the differences between the two and greatly underestimate similarities. David Brion Davis's study of slavery is a helpful resource here. In *The Problem of Slavery in Western Culture*, he discusses the issue of continuity in the history of servitude. He admits that slavery in North America possessed distinctive characteristics, such

47. Brown, *Introduction to New Testament*, 503–4.
48. Wilson, *Colossians and Philemon*, 328.

as its racial basis and legal barriers against manumission.[49] He even writes that it is necessary to make a distinction between slavery as an abstract legal status and as an actual institution with economic functions and interpersonal relationships.[50] Many New Testament scholars would agree with him. However, he makes a third point that they fail to identify. He claims that there is more institutional continuity between ancient and modern slavery than has been supposed. Even though slavery in America has marked differences in comparison with ancient slavery, "previous forms of servitude bore enough resemblance to the South's peculiar institution."[51]

There is a slight tendency for slave flight scholars to argue that ancient slavery was not as inhumane as American chattel slavery. There are even a few scholars who portray ancient slavery in complimentary terms. They admit that there were oppressive elements to ancient slavery but give considerable attention to positive aspects of slavery that ignore and soften its overall brutality. This does nothing more than legitimize the practice of slavery. For example, in *The Social Context of the New Testament*, Derek Tidball's comments about slavery are startling, and yet they reflect the opinion of too many New Testament scholars:

> In the first place, the institution of slavery was such an integral part of the social fabric in Paul's day that it would have been difficult for Paul or others to conceive of social organization without it. . . . By the time of Paul it was not a severe and cruel institution. Of course there were exceptions . . . but the experience of most slaves was different. In Carcopino's memorable phrase,

49. Davis, *Problem of Slavery*, 30.

50. Ibid.

51. Ibid., 31.

"with few exceptions slavery in Rome was neither eternal, nor, while it lasted . . . intolerable." . . . There was no widespread discontent about slavery. So, to the early church the question of the abolition of slavery was probably insignificant. . . . What Paul offers to Christian slaves is a totally new appreciation of their value as persons. They are no longer "things" but people who have standing and status before God (1 Cor 7:20). In Christ the slave is a free man. . . . If only, Paul argues, they grasp this greater fact, slavery becomes inconsequential. A slave can remain happily a slave and still serve the Lord in spite of his social limitations.[52]

Tidball's picture of slavery in the ancient world is deeply problematic for three reasons: his claims that slavery was not a cruel institution, that it was not intolerable, and that slaves were content and could even be happy with their condition. This is clearly an attempt to soften and sterilize the practice of slavery.

Another example comes from Lutheran scholar John G. Nordling, who scrutinizes the contemporary tendency among scholars who give too much attention to the brutality of Greco-Roman slavery.[53] Nordling thus sets out to provide a more "objective historical view of slavery" based on "evidence that . . . ancient slavery was not quite uniformly horrible."[54] Garland consents that slavery's essential nature corrodes the human spirit and yet also argues that ancient slavery was less beastly than new world slavery.[55] These scholars argue that there really is no need to

52. Tidball, *Social Context*, 114–16.

53. Dunn, *Epistles to the Colossians*, 306.

54. Nordling, *Philemon*, 43.

55. Garland, *Colossians, Philemon*, 348.

be morally repulsed by ancient slavery, negative elements notwithstanding. This is clearly problematic. It is important to understand some of the differences between ancient and modern slavery so as not to project modern ideas of race onto the slavery of the first century, but it is wrong to try to minimize ancient slavery. It may have offered limited benefit to a few but it left the majority disenfranchised, un-protected, vulnerable, and oppressed.

However, not all scholars subscribe to this belief. Scholars such as Clarice Martin, Allen Callahan, Brad Braxton, Mitzi J. Smith, and Jennifer Glancy strongly dis-agree with the idea that Greco-Roman slavery was not as oppressive as modern forms of slavery. Martin states, "The pervasive perception of ancient slavery as moderately stressful for the slave is historically naïve and ideologically presumptive."[56] This belief is naïve because, as Braxton ar-gues, even though "geographical location and ethnic and cultural factors might change from society to society, there are certain enduring sociological factors that are necessary and sufficient conditions for genuine slave societies such as ancient Rome."[57] Some scholars such as Smith want to go beyond the mere suggestion of similarities between ancient and modern slavery. She believes they are the same. She writes, "Slavery under the Roman Empire was no differ-ent from other slave societies in the cruel and inhumane treatment of slaves."[58] For example, she names the issue of violence and domination. The problem of violence, for "though (some) slaves could move upward socially, and thereby escape the violence at the lower levels of slavery,

56. Martin, "Somebody Done Hoodoo'd the Hodoo Man," 210–11.

57. Braxton, *Tyranny of Resolution*, 179.

58. Smith, "Slavery in the Early Church," in Blount et al, *True to Our Native Land*, 13.

this was the exception. Often in the imperial world slaves lived with the perpetual threat, as well as reality, of violence against which there was no legal recourse."[59] And, as Braxton found, "In the face of this violence, the slave had little legal recourse because in the eyes of Roman law slaves had no legal standing."[60] This is a qualitatively different picture than the one painted by scholars like Tidball, Garland, and Nordling.

Additionally, the personal domination of slaves by their masters is characteristic of slavery. Slaves were completely under the control of masters and lacked basic human and civil rights, such as dignity and honor. In her work on ancient slavery, Jennifer Glancy documented various accounts of violence, including rampant sexual abuse perpetrated against the bodies of slaves, and found that the law even permitted the casual abuse of slaves by freeborn persons who crossed their paths.[61] According to Glancy, "slaves' ambivalent legal status" opened the door for abuse.[62] Seneca, the Stoic philosopher, provided an account of slavery that seems to greatly support Glancy's contention. He remarks on the common belief that wealthy Romans thought it was degrading to dine with slaves. And as a result, Seneca offers this revealing portrait of Greco-Roman enslavement.

> It is only because purse-proud etiquette surrounds a house-holder at his dinner with a mob of standing slaves. The master eats more than he can hold . . . All this time the poor slaves may not move their lips, even to speak. The slightest murmur is repressed by the rod, even a chance

59. Braxton, *Tyranny of Resolution*, 186.

60. Ibid., 188.

61. Glancy, *Slavery in Early Christianity*, 13.

62. Ibid., 11.

> sound . . . a cough, a sneeze, or a hiccup . . . is
> visited with the lash. There is a grievous penalty
> for the slightest breach of silence. All night long
> they must stand about, hungry and dumb.[63]

This startling scene is a poignant reminder of the power-lessness, domination, and humiliation characterizing all forms of human enslavement, spanning the breadth of human history.

Scholars like Martin, Braxton, and Smith were influenced by Orlando Patterson's work on slavery. His seminal study on slavery proves that, although there are substantive differences between Greco-Roman slavery and American slavery, there are also substantive similarities. Patterson defines slavery as, "the permanent, violent domination of natally alienated and generally dishonored persons."[64] According to Patterson's study of slavery in Greece, Rome, medieval Europe, China, Korea, the Islamic kingdoms, Africa, the Caribbean Islands, and the American south, slavery has five common elements: the permanence of slavery; the violence of slavery; the personal domination of slaves; the natal alienation of slaves; and the dishonor of slaves. For Patterson, slavery in every era has been characterized by violence, humiliation, and control. Patterson's understanding of the common features of slavery is not accepted by many biblical scholars, especially interpreters of Philemon, who tend to focus on the complimentary aspects of slavery and the differences between ancient and modern slavery. This practice must be challenged and abandoned by New Testament scholars. Only then can we imagine anew the interpretation of this letter.

63. Seneca, "On Master and Slave."
64. Patterson, *Slavery and Social Death*, 13.

CONCLUSION

The web of exegetical, historical, cultural, and theological problems with the slave flight interpretation are deeply problematic and reflect a perspective that modern theology has long abandoned. The exclusive identification and alignment with the master class and not the enslaved goes against theological movements such as the Social Gospel, Catholic Social Teaching, and Liberation Theologies that privileges the position and perspective of the poor and marginalized. This kind of "slave-master" theology keeps the church blind to the realities and perspectives that come from the underside or other side of history. That is why theologians and more biblical scholars have long recognized the need to reorient its starting place and move away from perspectives rooted in Eurocentrism and colonialism.

The real problem with this interpretation is where it leaves the church. The exegetical, historical, cultural, and theological refusal to problematize the master-slave relationship hurts the witness of the church. Instead of using the letter to Philemon to wrestle earnestly with the challenges, promises, and complexities of living this faith in contexts where slavery and other forms of oppression are the norm, too many scholars are content to sanctify this norm and begin and end the theological task rationalizing the place and perspectives of the master class. This produces theology that rarely challenges the church to realign its witness among those who experience oppression and marginalization and reimagine a witness that moves the world closer to the reality of the kingdom of God. After all, the story and teachings in the text do not have to present a perfect picture of divine human relationality nor solve all the problems the text presents (slavery in the world). Rather, this story extends an invitation to wrestle anew with what they wrestled with in the first century. The interpretation of the letter to Philemon should reflect a theology that is honest about ways we fall short of giving witness of the kingdom of God. It challenges us to be courageous enough to envision how to live into the things that Christ's death and resurrection have made possible for the church and world. All of this and more are the kinds of theological musings that should preoccupy scholars of Philemon. As Philemon scholars, we must practice and embody a theology that upsets the social order instead of accommodating the Gospel to it. This is the kind of interpretive theology that represents the future of a church that is increasingly becoming more culturally and theologically diverse. And, more importantly, the absence of this kind of interpretation and theological reflection is a major reason the letter to Philemon is so often ignored by the church.

In the end, a real need to reimagine the interpretation of Philemon is clear. The church needs an interpretative orientation that does not Christianize or seek to legitimize slavery in any form, and more importantly, does not privilege the master class. Challenging the slave flight hypothesis will pave the way for scholars and the church to turn to Onesimus for an alternate interpretation of the letter to Philemon, imagining new possibilities and enlivening the witness of the church.

QUESTIONS FOR REFLECTION

1. What is the connection between the slave-flight interpretation and the problematic history of support for slavery by Christians for hundreds of years? Why it is an important part of the interpretation of Philemon?

2. The shadow of slavery hangs over the letter to Philemon. Why is it important to address problematic texts in the Bible with both critical honesty and humility while attempting to discern an interpretation that is faithful to the Gospel of Jesus Christ?

3. How should Christians respond to attempts by scholars and pastors to Christianize slavery using Philemon?

Chapter 2

Reimagining the Interpretation of Philemon

THE ONLY WAY MORE people of faith and scholars are going to read this book is if this letter's interpretation is reimagined in ways that spark interest and invite study. In my scholarship and teaching, I encourage people of faith and scholars to read and study this Pauline epistle with the kind of imagination and vision that strengthens and renews the witness of the church. Truthfully, there has been a tragic loss of creative thought as it relates to this small letter. The church and the academy have opted for the thieving, runaway slave interpretation, and, in return, failed to invite the church to explore both the historical importance of this letter in early Christianity and its theological depth if interpreted from a different perspective. But, there are signs of hope.

There has been a growing interest in the history and interpretation of this letter. As a result, new questions have arisen, leading to new interpretations of Philemon. It began with John Knox's controversial but highly important book,

Philemon Among the Letters of Paul, written in 1935. He imaginatively reconfigures relationships between the characters. First, Knox contends that Archippus was a deacon in Colossae while Philemon lived in Laodicea. Then, he suggests that Onesimus was the slave of Archippus and not Philemon. Third, he rejects the belief that Onesimus was a runaway. Instead, Knox argues that Paul was asking Archippus to give up his slave for Christian service. This would imply that Paul wrote the letter to Philemon so he could use his influence as a pastor in Colossae in this matter. Lastly, Knox claims that Onesimus was manumitted and later became the bishop of Ephesus, spoken of in Ignatius's letter to the Ephesians. Knox's work was so creative and challenging that it set the stage for debates that followed and intensified in the 1980s and '90s. In fact, between 1980 and 1999, nine journal articles opened new vistas in the interpretation of Philemon that significantly influenced commentaries and journal articles written from 2000 to the present.[1] Scholars have reimagined and vigorously debated the interpretation of Philemon and slowly began shifting the discourse in helpful ways for the church and the academy. Due to this original thinking, it is an exciting time to read and study Philemon.

WHY DID ONESIMUS LEAVE THE HOUSE?

In 1984, Sara Winter challenged the slave flight hypothesis. She reinterpreted this letter by using the work of John

1. Callahan, "Paul's Epistle to Philemon," 357–76; Callahan, "John Chrysostom on Philemon," 149–50; Lampe, "Keine Sklavenflucht des Onesimus." 135–37; Mitchell, "John Chrysostom on Philemon," 135–38; Nordling, "Onesimus Fugitivus," 97–119; Rapske, "Prisoner Paul," 187–203; Van Dyke, "Paul's Letter to Philemon," 384–98; Winter, "Methodological Observations," 203–12; Winter, "Paul's Letter to Philemon," 1–15.

Knox to construct an alternate picture of the relationship between Philemon, Paul, and Onesimus. Like Knox, Winter asserts that Archippus was the owner of the house where the church met and the master of Onesimus. Both Philemon and Apphia were church workers mentioned in v. 1. Winter claims that Onesimus was sent or dispatched to Paul, because the form of the letter showed Onesimus was with Paul bringing goods to the prisoners (Paul, Timothy, Epaphras). Instead of slave flight, she argues that Onesimus left the house because the church at Colossae sent him to minister to the imprisoned apostle.[2] This would mean, then, that the letter to Philemon was a legal petition for Onesimus's release from his obligations (vv. 8–14) and that he was no longer considered a slave within the church (v. 16–17). Furthermore, instead of paying for a slave's theft, v. 18 represents an offer to settle any debts Onesimus may have incurred while serving Paul.

Winter's dispatched-slave hypothesis has two strengths. It does not construct an interpretation based on the stereotype of the thieving slave but instead interprets Onesimus's role in the letter in a positive light. He was sent by the church to minister to Paul. It also makes better sense of the thanksgiving section (vv. 4–7), in which Paul is praising workers for love and generosity. This fits her interpretation better than the slave flight argument. However, there are weaknesses. First, Onesimus was not converted until leaving the house, and it is problematic that the church would dispatch a non-Christian to serve the imprisoned apostle. Second, Onesimus is referred to as useless in v. 11, a description that scholars understand to mean that he was not a good or profitable slave. And so, it is hard to imagine the church sending someone who was considered "useless" on a mission. These issues raise questions about her

2. Winter, "Methodological Observations," 203–12.

interpretation but in the end, her argument opens the door for others to reevaluate the letter's occasion.

Peter Lampe followed in 1985 with an alternate reason why Onesimus left the house. He argues that instead of Onesimus being sent to Paul, he sought out Paul to intercede between him and Philemon in a domestic dispute of some kind.[3] Unlike Winter's argument, Lampe's thesis was an extension of major tenets of the slave flight hypothesis in that it presupposed that Onesimus was the slave of Philemon and was at fault for stealing from his master, but it rejected the slave stereotype. He uses Roman legal texts to show that there were other reasons for slave flight. One notable example was when slaves would flee to a friend of the master to mediate a dispute, especially if they feared punishment of some kind. This is plausible and several scholars have begun to adopt a variation of this argument. For example, Brian Rapske discusses Proculus, a first century Roman jurist who claimed that "a slave is not a fugitive who, having in mind that his master wished to physically chastise him, betook himself to a friend who he induced to plead on his behalf."[4] What this suggests, then, is that it is still wrong to consider Onesimus as a fugitive slave because the reasons for flight were justifiable.

This particular interpretation opens the letter for deeper exploration by focusing on the condition of Onesimus's and Philemon's relationship. In Lampe's interpretation, Onesimus left the house after encountering some kind of domestic trouble with Philemon. He sought out Paul to intercede in the situation because a friend or mentor was more likely than a slave to calm a master's anger. Onesimus likely knew Paul because of his past interactions with

3. Lampe, "Keine Sklavenflucht des Onesimus," 135–37; Rapske, "Prisoner Paul," 187–203.

4. Rapske, "Prisoner Paul," 188–89, 96.

Philemon. Paul seems to suggest that Philemon became a Christian because of him in v. 19. It is also possible that Onesimus stole some money to facilitate the journey, which was why Paul promised to repay for any wrong or debt in v. 18. This hypothesis has much to commend because it raises the very real prospect that there was conflict between Philemon and Onesimus and this conflict was the reason Onesimus fled to Rome. It is also provides a viable explanation for the reason Onesimus was with Paul in prison, whereas the slave flight hypothesis has Onesimus meeting Paul by happenstance. Moreover, it also gives a reasonable explanation for Paul's promise to repay Philemon in v. 18. It is not based on the stereotype of a lazy and thieving slave. However, one weakness with Lampe's interpretation is that it does not discuss the issue of wrongdoing, either on the part of Philemon or Onesimus. In the letter, Paul does not explicitly accuse Philemon of wrongdoing or express Onesimus's remorse.

Winter and Lampe re-center the interpretation of Philemon because they refuse to accept the slave flight hypothesis with its problematic textual clues and slave stereotype. Instead, they offer different reasons for the departure of Onesimus. In fact, they make this the central interpretative issue of the letter: "Why did Onesimus leave the house?" In doing this, they open the door for scholars in the next two decades to begin to study the behavior and mindset of Philemon as the reason for Onesimus's departure.

RE-CENTERING THE INTERPRETATION OF PHILEMON

Even though the slave flight interpretation continues to be the primary way this letter is interpreted, we are seeing a slow process of re-centering the study as minority and

female scholars continue to expand the bounds of interpretation. African-American biblical scholars have made
important insights into the study and interpretation of Philemon that are a critical part of this new era in Philemon
studies. In particular, I stand on the shoulders of four gi-
ants in the field of African-American biblical interpretation
who have fueled my love of this small epistle.

Lloyd Lewis offers one of the first scholarly African-
American interpretations of Philemon. Even though he
confirms the problematic nature of the letter because of
its position on slavery, he chooses, instead, to focus on
the relationships between master and slave and the letter's
language. He contends that the relationship between Paul,
Philemon, and Onesimus was mitigated by Paul's careful
use of language that reinforced the image of the church as a
particular type of family. Lewis's work is important because
he makes three compelling arguments. First, he interprets
Paul's use of this language drawn from Gal 3:28 as not
only an attempt to communicate his wishes but actually
an attempt to modify Philemon's behavior. He argues that
language "helps to create or sustain social realities, which
was why he used family language in the letter."[5] Second,
he claims that Paul's use of the metaphor of the household
or family has the potential to effect sentiments that could
ideally change the nature of the relationship between Philemon and Onesimus. The implication is clear. Philemon
did not think of Onesimus in familial terms, and I suspect
this belief had very little to do with the fact that Onesimus
was not a Christian and more to do with him being a slave.
The reality that Onesimus became a Christian does change
things. Lewis adds, "The old structures of subordination no
longer hold for those who are baptized . . . where all are

5. Lewis, "African American Appraisal," in Felder, *Stony the Road
We Trod*, 233–34.

considered as one and therefore peers."[6] This metaphor was so important that he poignantly concludes that the letter reflects Paul's belief in shared status or mutuality. So, the purpose of the letter to Philemon was to use careful language to transform Philemon's understanding of his relationship with this slave.

Clarice Martin goes further than Lewis's focus on language by focusing on Paul's use of rhetoric, particularly what she identifies as commercial language in v. 18: "if he wronged you or owes you anything, I will repay." She believes that Paul was advocating for the emancipation of Onesimus. By drawing on the work of F. Forrester Church, Martin carefully examines Paul's use of deliberative rhetoric, a type of rhetoric that seeks to effect the expedient and advantageous at a future time.[7] It may be used either in advice given in private, or during public speaking to an assembly. Deliberative rhetoric has three divisions: exordium, main body or proof, and peroration, each seeking, to some extent, to fulfill a desired action in future time. For example, the exordium excites or removes prejudice and magnifies or minimizes the importance of the subject. For Martin, Philemon resembles this style of writing. Paul's prologue and opening prayer in vv. 1–7 are the exordium that "strives to secure Philemon's favor by introducing the motifs of love, good, and partnership in such a way that they redound to Philemon's credit."[8] In the main body, ethos, pathos, and logos are employed in reference to Philemon's good character. The appeal to providence in verses 15–16 reframes the departure of Onesimus in a way that influences Philemon in this matter. On this point Martin notes, "The reception of Onesimus as a brother, then, would represent

6. Ibid., 239.

7. Church, "Rhetorical Structure," 1–18.

8. Martin, "Commercial Language," 326.

the completion of God's design."[9] In the peroration, verses 17–20, Paul's request for Onesimus finds not only its clearest expression but possibly its most profound. Paul asks Philemon to receive Onesimus as if he were the beloved apostle. The use of "partner" in v. 17 "serves to illicit loyalty and goodwill, and provides a motive for Philemon to respond."[10] Paul's invocation of partnership sets the stage for anticipation, addressing the objections before they were given to rectify them or set them aside. Martin's analysis of Paul's use of rhetoric to effect change in Philemon is an important contribution to Philemon studies because it focuses on Philemon as the one Paul was trying to change.

Cain H. Felder's commentary on Philemon in the New Interpreters Bible series is another compelling contribution to the interpretation of this letter by an African-American scholar. For Felder, the letter to Philemon was a "plea for a renewed relationship between the two, but on better terms than before in light of their mutual faith as Christians."[11] He ardently disagrees that the primary focus of the letter was the slavery issue. Instead, he contends that "the central meaning and purpose of the letter to Philemon concern the difference the transforming power of the gospel can make in the lives and relationships of believers regardless of class or other distinctions."[12] Felder's insights highlight class and social distinction issues that influenced the events that led to Onesimus's departure and Paul's letter of appeal.

Imagine a different relationship between Philemon and Onesimus. Allen D. Callahan introduces a strong case for calling the supposed flight of Onesimus into question. He asserts that the epistle states Onesimus ran away. In fact,

9. Ibid., 328.

10. Ibid., 329.

11. Felder, "Philemon," in Keck, *New Interpreter's Bible*, 884.

12. Ibid.

he rejects the idea that Onesimus was a slave. He proposes, instead of the master-slave relationship, Philemon and Onesimus were actually estranged Christian brothers in need of Paul's mediation.[13] This belief is based on his interpretation of "no longer as a slave but a brother in the flesh and in the Lord" in v. 16. Callahan believes this means they share both a blood relationship and now a Christian relationship. The reference to a slave was "the antitype of a blood relative" because it was a world where slaves experienced "natal alienation" and because, in the writings of Paul, slavery was a metaphor for familial alienation.[14] This point is important because Paul's use of slave language in this and other writings is metaphorical. Therefore, there is no need to think Onesimus was a literal slave, and Paul is simply addressing Philemon's view of his brother. Callahan believes Paul was challenging Philemon to stop treating his brother as a slave. There may be some benefit to reimagining the relationship between Philemon as master and Onesimus as slave but the evidence in the letter does not seem to fit this reconfiguration. Familial language in Philemon is metaphorical whereas the language of slave in v. 16 seems literal. Callahan's work is important in that it provides a new way to interpret the letter but what I find to be the most significant point made is his belief that Paul was challenging Philemon to discontinue the mistreatment of Onesimus.

There are white scholars who have also been pushing the boundaries in the interpretation of Philemon. One notable scholar has explored the possibility that Paul was rebuking Philemon. Robert Van Dyke has taken a critical posture against Philemon and the church for its failure to address that Onesimus was an unconverted Christian. He asserts, "It could well be that Paul's appeal on behalf of

13. Callahan, *Embassy*, 1–19.
14. Callahan, "Paul's Epistle to Philemon," 370.

Onesimus was a wake-up call to Philemon and others at the house . . . about what they were doing," and he poignantly asks, "Why did Paul have to convert Onesimus?"[15] For Van Dyke, in v. 6, "Hidden in the lauds and thanksgivings he is heaping upon Philemon and the church, Paul targeted Philemon with a sort of left jab in disguise." This verse implied that Paul's prayer for Philemon's sharing to become effectual was an indication that it had not been effectual, especially regarding Onesimus. Moreover, Van Dyke views the entire letter as a "means to make a statement about the need for Philemon to refresh his ministry, his mission, and his outlook on people right under his own roof."[16]

Craig De Vos focuses on manumission and relational patterns in the letter. He writes, "One of the most difficult interpretive issues in the letter to Philemon has been what Paul was actually asking Philemon to do."[17] Some interpreters believe it was ultimately manumission, to release Onesimus from being a slave of Philemon. But De Vos questions whether that would really change anything between Philemon as master and Onesimus as slave. This question identifies the deeper problem that this letter exposes, the effects of problematic relational patterns in Greco-Roman households. This is an issue completely ignored by the slave flight interpretation. These patterns were likely an important part of the events that shaped the occasion of Paul's letter to Philemon. One example De Vos notes was what he called the "stereotyped slave personality."

> In support of this we find a stereotyped slave personality, commonly held and espoused by the elite, that slaves were by definition lazy, negligent, willful, cowardly, and criminals. There is

15. Van Dyke, "Paul's Letter to Philemon," 391.
16. Ibid., 392.
17. De Vos, "Once a Slave, Always a Slave," 89.

a similar stereotyped slave persona found in the caricature of slaves in Greek comedy, a caricature that could only work if there was some basis in reality. So, for example, Menander portrays slaves as scheming and deceitful, negligent and insolent.[18]

Stereotypes like these in the minds of elites cause De Vos to believe that manumission would not have changed the relationship between Philemon and Onesimus because it was likely that Philemon held similar beliefs about slaves. Paul was trying to address the perceptional problem and not just the structural problem. Until Paul challenged Philemon at the level of perception, the structural level would have been superfluous. "Paul wanted the relationship to take on the character of a filial relationship . . . shift from slave to brother."[19] That is why the language of a brother in the flesh and in the Lord in v. 16 was important, because "in the flesh" is a reference to relationships in the household setting, while "in the Lord" refers to relationships within the church setting. While they were clearly not social equals—Philemon was the master and Onesimus was the slave—Paul was attempting to cause a fundamental change in this relationship to the extent that they view one another as equals.

These two writings are important because they suggest the possibility that Philemon's perception and treatment of Onesimus resembled views held by other households. Philemon may even have believed those stereotypes about slaves being lazy, negligent, and cowardly, and treated Onesimus based on those false beliefs. More importantly, it suggests that these attitudes are the very things Paul was

18. Ibid., 95.
19. Ibid., 102.

seeking to correct in vv. 6, 11, and to shift in vv. 16–17 in the mind of Philemon.

These scholars have successfully advanced the interpretation of Philemon beyond the limited bounds of the slave flight interpretation. They imagine new angles in interpretation and chart new paths for others to follow. Modern New Testament students and scholars should continue to draw on these works as they envision different and deeper ways to interpret the letter to Philemon. I have found their work to be helpful as an African-American interpreter of the Bible and this letter.

These scholars develop four instrumental arguments. First, Paul did not mention the flight of Onesimus. I agree with Winter and Callahan that the thanksgiving section of the letter in vv. 4–7 does not fit the flight hypothesis and the motive for flight is obscure. There are good reasons for interpreters to stop reading flight into the letter. Second, in Winter, Lampe, and Callahan's interpretations, Onesimus knew Paul. Either he was sent to Paul to minister to him, to seek his help in resolving a dispute of some kind, or they were estranged brothers. Lampe's interpretation that there was some kind of dispute or tension that caused Onesimus to leave the house and intentionally seek out Paul is most plausible. Third, African-American scholars have pointed to Paul's writing using familial or filial language and rhetoric aimed at correcting Philemon's understanding of his relationship to Onesimus. Though many use the slave flight hypothesis, they agree that this relational misunderstanding was the cause of the entire situation. And finally, Van Dyke's bold work opens the door to the most important exegetical issue in the letter, namely the fact that Onesimus was not converted to the faith while a slave in Philemon's house. It is problematic that Onesimus did not come to faith until meeting with Paul in prison. Verse 6 is a carefully worded and mild critique of Philemon's treatment of Onesimus using the word koinōnia, which can be translated as fellowship, sharing, or participation.

THE EXCLUSIONARY
KOINONIA INTERPRETATION

I propose new way to view this letter that deals with the issues of exclusion and koinōnia (fellowship). My hope is that readers will find it illuminating and helpful, being inspired to read and study Philemon anew. There is compelling evidence for this interpretation at both the exegetical, historical, theological, and cultural levels. My aim in the rest of this companion is to make the case for this new approach.

The first step requires a different historical occasion (or back story). In the following I share at length what I have written elsewhere. My hope is that it will open the letter to Philemon in many helpful ways.

> Philemon, a leader in the church at Colossae, is committed to the work of the gospel. In fact, Paul has heard how beneficial Philemon has been in the church "refreshing the hearts of the saints." However, Philemon has limited his understanding of fellowship because he does not extend it to his slaves. In the eyes of Philemon, slaves are useless, only fit for miscellaneous tasks in his household. Philemon occasionally mistreats and even abuses his slaves for not performing duties properly. It is clear that Philemon has little regard for slaves in the household. One slave in particular named Onesimus is strong-willed and dislikes the treatment his fellow slaves receive at the hands of Philemon. Much to the dismay of his fellow slaves, Onesimus even confronted

Philemon about the issue but it did not change how he viewed and treated his slaves.

Over the course of time, the relationship between Philemon and Onesimus has become contentious. Onesimus feels that Philemon is hypocritical in showing generosity to the saints and not to his slaves. In fact, while some slaves have become Christians, Onesimus has refused to accept this distorted form of religion and told his friends that Christianity was a sham. One particular afternoon, Christians from the community gathered to share the bread and cup. Philemon had the slaves prepare the meal but forbade them from participating with the others. After seeing this, Onesimus became angry and again confronted Philemon. Being embarrassed by the confrontation, Philemon threatened to punish his slave severely. Fearing punishment, Onesimus left (possibly taking money to facilitate travel) and sought out Paul in the hope that the imprisoned apostle would intercede on his behalf. Onesimus knew of Paul through Philemon, Apphia, and Archippus. Onesimus shared his story with Paul. Much to his surprise, he found Paul to be loving and welcoming. For the first time he felt respected and accepted as a person, and not just a slave. Days later, in a cold prison, God's love finally broke through the social barriers of the day and touched his wounded heart. Shortly thereafter, Onesimus became a Christian and received the bread and cup from the apostle himself. So inspired by God's work in his life, he immediately began to help Paul. The imprisoned apostle became extremely fond of the sincere zeal, energy, and giftedness employed to meet the apostle's needs as he served other churches.

Knowing that Onesimus was legally bound to return to his master, and also wanting to effect reconciliation, Paul penned this mediatory letter which was to be delivered to Philemon by Onesimus. He had two primary concerns in mind: to offer some word concerning Onesimus, and more importantly, to speak a word to Philemon and the church at Colossae about the kind of koinōnia that can transform this broken relationship between master and slave. As a result, Paul requests that Philemon's capacity for fellowship be expanded so as to include the slaves in his household and Onesimus who has returned with the letter. Paul also requests that Philemon welcomes Onesimus as a beloved brother and no longer only as a slave. Furthermore, he promises that if Philemon has been wronged the apostle himself will repay him when next they meet. Lastly, it also appears that Paul mildly suggests that Philemon allow Onesimus to return to Paul to continue helping him in prison, or even manumit him altogether. Paul is confident that Philemon, who has already demonstrated a capacity to refresh the hearts of saints, will do this and more, especially considering how God has worked to give him a broader understanding of koinōnia.[20]

This is clearly a different picture of the situation that influenced the writing of the letter to Philemon. It does not fit the slave flight interpretation.

In my approach to Philemon, the seminal question of the letter is why Onesimus was an unconverted slave in the house of a Christian master (v. 10). The central issue of the letter was the failure of another early Christian leader to include people considered "outsiders" in some sense. This

20. Brogdon, "Exclusion as Impediment to Conversion," 117–18.

was a problem Paul had encountered before with Peter, Barnabas, certain men associated with James, and even the church at Corinth. The selective sharing of fellowship and food was a problem in early Christian communities, and Paul consistently challenged this kind of duplicity and hypocrisy. Philemon was in the wrong and it was possibly even a problem in the Colossian church, which was already heavily influenced by religious forces in the culture there (Col 2:8–23). Exclusion, selective inclusion, or ineffectual fellowship was the problem, and I contend this was the reason Onesimus was not converted in the house of Philemon. He was viewed as a "useless slave" (v. 11) and excluded from the fellowship Philemon extended to those Philemon considered "saints" vv. 6–7. Onesimus's experience of exclusion and treatment as "a slave," or as I prefer to translate this verse as "just a slave" (v. 16), was an impediment to conversion.

Being viewed in this manner could force us to consider that Philemon was an abusive or harsh master, an issue Paul addressed with this church in Col 4:1. So it is possible that Onesimus left the house for either being consistently excluded or threatened by Philemon. He sought out Paul to mediate the situation. Paul's belief that social and religious distinctions like Jew or Hebrew, Greek, Pharisee, circumcised, slave, free, male, female were meaningless in light of the work of Christ. He practiced this belief by treating Onesimus as a brother (Gal 3:28; Phil 3:2–10). The imprisoned apostle's love for one considered "useless" became the impetus for his conversion. The letter to Philemon, therefore, represents Paul's intervention in the matter (vv. 8–10). In the letter, he requested Philemon's "fellowship of faith" be broadened ("active" or "effectual" v. 6) to include Onesimus. He challenged Philemon to reconsider the assessment Onesimus was "useless" in light of his conversion and valued by the imprisoned apostle (vv. 11–12). Paul, therefore, made two explicit requests and one implicit request. First, he asked that Onesimus no longer be viewed as just a slave who was excluded from the fellowship (v. 16). Second, he asked that Onesimus be received by Philemon and the congregation as a beloved brother in the Lord (vv. 16–17). The first two requests address both how Onesimus would be perceived and how he would be treated in the future. Paul was clearly making correctives to Philemon's, and possibly the church's behavior. Implicitly, Paul framed his remarks in a way that, in order for Philemon and the church to follow them, Onesimus must have been allowed to return to Paul and possibly freed altogether. Paul left the issue of manumission to the discretion of Philemon, but implicitly exerted a great deal of moral pressure on Philemon to comply (vv. 13–14, 20–22).

This interpretation of Philemon offers the following strengths. First, it is based on textual evidence. There are five exegetical clues in vv. 6, 10, 11, 16, and 17 supporting this interpretation: "(I pray) that the fellowship of your faith may become effective through knowledge of every good thing in us through Christ" (v. 6); "I appeal to you concerning my child Onesimus, whom I have begotten while imprisoned" (v. 10); "Formerly he was useless to you but now he is useful to me and to you" (v. 11); "No longer as just a slave but more than a slave, a beloved brother, especially to me and much more to you both as a person and in the Lord" (v. 16); "and therefore if you regard me as a partner, receive him as you would receive me" (v. 17). Second, it connects to problems other leaders and congregations faced in the first century. They struggled with the radical and inclusive nature of the gospel. Duplicity and hypocrisy are central issues. The problem is very Pauline. Next, it connects with the treatment of house slaves in first-century, extra-biblical sources, and explicit teaching on it in New Testament letters. Fourth, it provides a better explanation of Onesimus's failure to be converted, his departure and resultant meeting with Paul, Paul's promise to pay Philemon for any loss, and the careful rhetoric of the letter. Finally, it opens the letter up for theological considerations that strengthen and challenge the church's witness in the world.

There are also noted weaknesses to this interpretation. Paul did not explicitly say that Philemon mistreated Onesimus. He even complimented him: "I give thanks to my God always making mention of you in my prayers when I hear of your love and faith which you have toward the Lord Jesus Christ and all the saints" (vv. 4–5). He suggested the possibility that was inferred in vv. 6, 10, 11, 16–17, and 22.

> (I pray) that the fellowship of your faith may become effective through knowledge of every good thing in us through Christ. . . . I appeal to you concerning my child Onesimus, whom I have begotten while imprisoned. . . .Formerly he was useless to you but now he is useful to me and to you. . . . No longer as just a slave but more than a slave, a beloved brother, especially to me and much more to you both as a person and in the Lord . . . and therefore if you regard me as a partner, receive him as you would receive me. . . . And also prepare me a lodging for I hope that through your prayers I shall be released to you.

Another weakness is linguistic in nature. I interpret v. 11 literally and as an actual reference to how Philemon viewed him and not as a statement of fact, and I translate v. 16 as best understood to say "not just as a slave." This expression captures the essence and nuance of what Paul was saying. Slave flight scholars interpret v. 11 as a statement about

Onesimus's performance as a slave or a pun. They also do not add the phrase "just as a slave" but translate it "as a slave." The obvious weakness is that my interpretation depends on the most obscure verse of the letter, v. 6, which includes a very ambiguous phrase. In fact, this is one of the most ambiguous phrases in Paul's writings. Normally it is best not to construct an interpretation using an obscure verse, but there is no reason to make this a hard rule without exception. I hope to show this verse, though obscure, is important to Paul's carefully worded letter and deserves equal interpretative weight.

The exclusionary koinōnia interpretation is not perfect but it is plausible, at least as plausible as the slave flight interpretation. It connects with major themes in other studies of this letter. It also recalibrates the letter's focus away from the master, Philemon, and to the slave, Onesimus, who had an interesting history in the early church that has long been neglected.

RECOVERING THE ANCIENT ROOTS OF PHILEMON AND ITS INCLUSION IN THE CANON

I believe it is good news for the church to read Philemon in a way other than through the lens of an escaped slave being returned to his master. Similar to Sarah Winter's work, I return to John Knox's study, which paved a way to reorient the focus of the letter from the master to the slave. This reading is liberating message to marginalized peoples. Though Knox's conclusions are not new, his study takes up the issue of the letter's inclusion in the canon, which for me, is an important place to begin. The letter was often named in the lists of Pauline letters; however, it was not regarded as having any theological value. So why does it appear in lists of Pauline letters and why was it later included in the canon? After all, Philemon is a brief letter and does not appear as substantive as other Pauline letters, such as Romans, the Corinthian correspondence, or Galatians. Indeed, the letter's brevity and the fact that it is a private letter caused leaders in the early church to question why it was included in the canon. For example, Jerome, a fourth century priest and theologian, believed in comparison with other Pauline letters, Philemon was trivial.

Knox suggests the inclusion of Philemon was primarily due to it being regarded as an authentic Pauline letter often associated with the letter to the Colossians. There are eight persons found in both Philemon and Colossians, which reinforces the letters authenticity. More importantly, he focuses on the role of Onesimus in this history. Knox offers some compelling arguments that indirectly shift the interpretive focus of this letter away from Philemon to Onesimus. He argues that in the letter to Philemon, Paul was asking Archippus to give up his slave for Christian service, that Onesimus was manumitted, and that he later became the bishop of Ephesus spoken of in Ignatius's letter to the Ephesians. Onesimus also played a vital role in collecting Paul's letters into a corpus and included Paul's letter to Philemon in the corpus since it spoke of him. This is a significant and overlooked part of the history of Philemon. Knox raised the possibility that the reason or reasons the letter was included in the canon and its importance for the church goes beyond its authenticity as a Pauline letter. Knox suggested that Onesimus gathered the letters of Paul into a corpus to give some rationale for Philemon's inclusion in the canon. I believe the story of Onesimus is a major reason for the letter's inclusion and importance for the church. The idea that Onesimus, a former slave, became a bishop in Ephesus is radical and worthy of further exploration.

Though only a very small part of the history of the letter to Philemon, this is a big deal. The remote possibility that Onesimus's story was the reason the letter was included in the canon is a powerful piece of church history. The ascent from an unconverted house slave of a formerly duplicitous Christian master to a converted Christian through the Apostle Paul who later became a bishop of one of the major churches in early Christendom is incredibly compelling and inspiring. Yet it is a narrative that the church has rejected and or ignored for a dominant interpretation based on problematic inferences, stereotypes, and centuries of pain. The big question is, "How do we know Onesimus became a bishop in Ephesus?" The answer is that we do not know if it is true. It is, however, a part of the history of the letter. One of the church fathers, Ignatius of Antioch, raised this possibility in a letter to the Ephesians. Ignatius was born in 35 CE and served as the third Bishop of Antioch. He was believed to have studied under the Apostle John. Ignatius was also an influential thinker in the early church, being an early advocate for the deity of Christ and the universality of the church. He was arrested and died in Rome as a martyr.

In Ignatius's letter to the Ephesians, there are at least fourteen references to Onesimus. For example, Ignatius writes, "Ye were eager to visit me: seeing then that in God's name I have received your whole multitude in the person of Onesimus, whose love passeth utterance and who is moreover your bishop [in the flesh] and I pray that ye may love him according to Jesus Christ and that ye all may be like him; for blessed is He that granted unto you according to your deserving to have such a bishop."[21] This is one example of the many laudatory claims made by Ignatius regarding Onesimus, who travelled to Smyrna to visit him with other

21. Ignatius, "Letter to the Ephesians" in Lightfoot and Harner, *Apostolic Fathers*, 137.

representatives from the Ephesian church: Burrhus, Crocus, Euplus, and Fronto. It is highly significant that both the Apostle Paul and Ignatius were overwhelmingly complimentary in their description of Onesimus. We can deduce from the earliest witnesses of the church—Paul's letters to the Colossians and Philemon and Ignatius's letter to the Ephesians—that Onesimus was a man of great faith, love, and service to the church, a testimony that was warped by a hypothesis that accused him of being a thieving runaway.

Not all scholars believe that the Onesimus mentioned in Philemon is the same Onesimus in Ignatius's letter to the Ephesians. Fitzmyer says that it is a possibility and "no more than that," since this claim has been made in commentaries dating back to Chrysostom.[22] Others believe it is speculative at best because the name Onesimus was so common in ancient documents and inscriptions. I agree with Fitzmyer. It is a possibility, one worth considering as I attempt to reimagine the interpretation of this letter. Considering that the usual suppositions concerning the flight of Onesimus and his apparent theft are also speculative, we can also consider the possibility that Onesimus was the bishop of Ephesus, mentioned by Ignatius. Inferences about Onesimus as a fugitive slave have buttressed an oppressive interpretation of Philemon for cenuries. Why not use inference in a way that provides a liberating interpretation?

Why is this narrative important? The story of Onesimus becoming a bishop is a part of the story of early Christendom. Whether or not it is true, it is important as a historical issue and as a theological issue. This story was an important part of the Pauline tradition. It is certainly a better place to begin interpreting this letter than what is offered by the slave flight hypothesis. This narrative sheds new light on our understanding of the significance of the letter

22. Fitzmyer, *Letter to Philemon*, 15.

to Philemon. This short letter details the messy intersection between slavery in the Greco-Roman world and slavery in Christian households. Through this one incident, the letter introduces us to the challenges that early Christians faced as their beliefs and practices began to take shape. Luke T. Johnson views Philemon as a carefully crafted witness of an emerging Christian ethos, showing both its power to transform symbols and attitudes and its struggle to transcend social forms.[23] Johnson's point suggests Christian beliefs were still developing. Their understanding of the implications of the gospel were evolving as they encountered challenges like enslaved persons. One of the early challenges in the church was the institution of slavery and the slaves who would encounter the liberating and subversive power of the gospel.

This narrative also helps biblical interpreters, theologians, and historians make sense of the tenuous link between the church and slavery. It reflects both a church struggling with faith questions as it relates to slavery and anticipating future struggles in the church with these same issues. The tensions between Philemon and Onesimus would plague the church for two millennia. In this letter, we encounter the church's struggle with a radical gospel and a tendency toward social conservatism that allowed it to justify oppressive institutions and practices. The book of Philemon tells two stories about the church as it relates to slavery. Some people in the church, like Philemon, would accommodate themselves to oppressive institutions for their own benefit while exploiting others. They would actively participate in excluding others and even perpetrate violence, blind to their problematic behavior. Yet in spite of this, others in the church, like Onesimus, would reject an accommodating gospel and experience a liberating gospel

23. Johnson, *Writings of the New Testament*, 387.

in strange places, even spaces outside churches. In some instances, those persons would become leaders in the same church that formerly oppressed them. Influential leaders in the church, like Paul in this letter, would have to raise their voice and use their influence to challenge those who stood on the wrong side of justice, calling the world and the church to account. What a reversal of the slave flight interpretation of this letter! I situate my interpretation within the larger context of the early church's struggle to live into the radical nature of the gospel.

CONCLUSION:
A MODERN STORY OF ONESIMUS

The exclusionary koinōnia interpretation of Philemon resonates with marginalized communities in the church. It offers an additional cultural benefit as they work with majority communities in the church to imagine better ways to give witness to the gospel. Because this interpretation centralizes Onesimus, it provides a way for historically marginalized peoples to enter this story in the Bible and this history in the church, a history that is painful yet instructive. This cultural benefit is needed because there are Onesimus's in our traditions and churches that we need to identify, learn from, and centralize. For example, one of the black church's historic denominations, the African Methodist Episcopal (AME) Church, has a founder with a story similar to the one of Onesimus in the letter to Philemon. Both men went from slavery to becoming bishops in the church and both experienced exclusion from Christian leaders (and congregations). Richard Allen was born a slave of Benjamin Chew in Philadelphia in 1760. He spent his formative years on a plantation in Dover Delaware belonging to Mr. Stokely. In 1777, Allen had a conversion experience that influenced him to become a minister. The experience catalyzing his exodus from the Methodist Episcopal Church to what later became the African Methodist Episcopal (A. M. E.) Church was an incident of exclusion that occurred at St. George's Methodist Episcopal Church. Allen and Absalom Jones were freed slaves and yet in the church they were continually excluded and marginalized. His famous account of his friend who was interrupted while praying offers an interesting parallel to what I believe happened to Onesimus. Allen recalled,

> We had not been long upon our knees before I heard considerable scuffling and low talking. I raised my head up and saw Mr. H_ M_, having hold of the Rev. Absalom Jones, pulling him off his knees and saying, "You must get up . . . you must not kneel here." Mr. Jones replied, "Wait until prayer is over." Mr. H_ M_ said, "No you must get up now, or I will call for aid and force you away." Mr. Jones said, "Wait until prayer is over, and I will get up and trouble you no more." With that he beckoned to one of the other trustees, Mr. L_ S_ to come to his assistance. He came, and went to William White to pull him up. By this time prayer was over, and we all went out of the church in a body, and they were no more plagued with us in the church.[24]

The image of someone being interrupted while praying in a church by people who professed to be Christian is poignant and deeply painful to imagine. No one would blame Allen, Jones, and others for leaving that congregation.

Yet there is something instructive in this, because exclusion does not have the final word for people like

24. Allen, "Life Experience and Gospel Labors," in Sernett, *African American Religious History*, 146

Onesimus and Richard Allen. The more compelling aspect of this story is not the incident of exclusion but rather the resilience of Allen and others to find space where they could worship. Their steadfast commitment to Christian faith persisted despite how the whites in St. George's embodied Christianity. The Spirit was with Richard Allen and Absalom Jones and was at work in the situation. Years later, Allen became the first bishop in the Methodist Episcopal Church and one of the most influential leaders in American Protestantism. Both Onesimus and Allen were slaves and later became bishops in the church. They were set on the path to liberation and church leadership from an experience of exclusion by Christian leaders.

The truth is that there are a lot of stories like this in minority traditions that can challenge the church to be honest about our history of exclusion and inspire us to participate in Spirit movements that counteract this history. In the end, constructive interpretation helps the church and academy reimagine the meaning of Christian witness amidst the fallen structures of the world. The next step is to move to the exegetical study of the letter, examining the textual basis for my interpretation that Paul was challenging Philemon to radically change both his view and treatment of slaves.

QUESTIONS FOR REFLECTION

1. Why have interpreters ignored the fact that Onesimus was an unconverted slave in the house of a Christian master and its bearing on the interpretation of the letter? Why is the location of his conversion so important?

2. In what ways does the exclusionary koinōnia theory advance an interpretation that speaks to issues like liberation from oppression, empowerment of marginalized

persons, restoration of fractured relationships, and healing from the dehumanizing pain of oppression?

3. What are some of the major theories about the historical
occasion behind the letter to Philemon? How do these
theories address the four key issues in the letter?
   a. The nature of the relationship between Philemon
      and Onesimus
   b. Why Onesimus was with Paul in prison
   c. Why Onesimus was converted to the faith in
      prison with Paul and not in the household of
      Philemon
   d. What Paul was asking Philemon to do about
      Onesimus

Chapter 3

Exclusionary Koinonia: A New Interpretation of Philemon

INSTEAD OF THE LETTER to Philemon addressing a pilfering runaway slave who was returned to his good master, I offer an alternate interpretation. Rooted in a different back story, my interpretation is consistent with the text, with practices in first-century households, and with first-century churches. It provides a firm foundation to address theological issues of exclusion like racism, classism, sexism, and their intersections with how Christian churches understand and practice koinōnia. The exclusionary koinōnia interpretation focuses on the subjugation and discrimination of Onesimus by Philemon as the cause of his departure. I also shine a light on the timeline of Onesimus's conversion. He was an unconverted slave in the house of a Christian master. Paul was concerned with the issue of exclusion and framed it through the lens of koinōnia in v. 6.

This letter has to be read with four considerations in mind. Paul was being careful in his writing because Onesimus would return with the letter and was in a vulnerable position, facing possible punishment if Philemon felt embarrassed or dishonored. Paul's phrasing and word choice were very intentional. Philemon had the power to welcome or punish his departed slave and there was nothing Paul or Onesimus could do to stop him. Second, Paul was subversively siding with Onesimus and challenged both Philemon and the church to transform. Third, he was being as confrontational as possible from the vantage point of a prison in Rome. Paul was correcting the beliefs and practices in Philemon and the church that obstructed the way of salvation for Onesimus. Paul did not want to embarrass or humiliate Philemon but he was trying to correct him. Fourth, Paul was leveraging the goodwill he had with Philemon (vv. 17–20). He leveraged his personal and apostolic relationship with Philemon to correct and encourage him to live into the change he laid out for him in vv. 16–17.

TRANSLATION OF THE LETTER TO PHILEMON

1 Paul a prisoner of Christ Jesus and Timothy our brother to Philemon our beloved brother and fellow worker, 2 and to Apphia our sister and Archippus our fellow soldier and to the church that meets in your house. 3 Grace to you and peace from God our Father and the Lord Jesus Christ. 4 I give thanks to my God always making mention of you in my prayers 5 when I hear of your love and faith which you have toward the Lord Jesus Christ and all the saints. 6 (I pray) that the fellowship of your faith may become effective through knowledge of every good thing in us through Christ. 7 For I have much joy and comfort from your love because the hearts of the saints have been refreshed through you, brother. 8 Although I have much boldness in Christ to

order you to do what is right. 9 But rather I appeal to you in love, Paul, being an old man and now a prisoner of Christ Jesus. 10 I appeal to you concerning my child Onesimus, whom I have begotten while imprisoned. 11 Formerly he was useless to you but now he is useful to me and to you, 12 whom I send back to you, that is, my very heart. 13 I wished that I could keep him with me that he might minister to me on your behalf in the bonds of the gospel. 14 But I would not do anything without your consent so that your good is not done by necessity but rather willingly. 15 For perhaps he was separated for a time so that you might have him back forever. 16 No longer as just a slave but more than a slave, a beloved brother, especially to me and much more to you both as a person and in the Lord. 17 Therefore if you regard me as a partner, receive him as you would receive me. 18 And if he wronged you or owes you anything, charge it to me. 19 I, Paul, am writing this with my hand, I will repay it; not to mention that you owe me your very self. 20 Yes brother, I want some benefit from you in the Lord, refresh my heart in Christ. 21 Being confident of your obedience, I wrote to you knowing that you will go beyond what I ask. 22 And also prepare me a lodging for I hope that through your prayers I shall be released to you. 23 Greet Epaphras my fellow prisoner in Christ Jesus. 24 Mark, Aristarchus, Demas, Luke, my fellow workers. 25 The grace of the Lord Jesus Christ be with your spirit.

GREETINGS FROM PAUL TO PHILEMON VV. 1–3

Paul opens this letter referring to himself as a "prisoner of Christ Jesus," a phrase also used in Eph 3:1 and Phil 1:1, which is why the letter to Philemon is one of prison epistles. He often calls himself an "apostle of Christ Jesus" in his letters (1 Cor 1:1; 2 Cor 1:1; Gal 1:1; Eph 1:1; Col 1:1; 1 Tim 1:1; and 2 Tim 1:1), and occasionally "a slave of Jesus Christ" (Rom 1:1; Phil 1:1; and Titus 1:1). Both an apostle of Christ Jesus and a slave of Christ would have been appropriate but Paul opted for a prisoner of Christ, a phrase only used in the prologue of this letter. Paul's phrasing sets a particular tone in a subversive letter that seeks to correct the recipient. Paul was suffering for the gospel, and the phrase elicits a degree of sympathy. It is also an important instructional motif about Christian vocation. There is a literal meaning connected to his arrest and imprisonment in Rome. Paul was literally "a prisoner of Christ." There is also a deeper figurative and theological meaning. Paul was "a prisoner for the sake of Christ," which recognizes his crime, preaching the gospel. As a prisoner, he was not free. His choices had limits. This would be an important issue because Onesimus would do things he may not have wanted to do and Philemon would be asked to do things he might not have wanted to do. Paul invited them both to see themselves as prisoners of Christ.

Another layer to the subversive nature of the letter is Paul making this a congregational issue, indirectly making it public. The letter to Philemon was not a private letter. For example, Paul was not alone in writing it. Timothy was mentioned in v. 1 as "our brother" and co-author. He was a valued member of Paul's apostolic ministry. In fact, he was mentioned as co-author of three additional undisputed letters (1 Thessalonians, Philippians, 2 Corinthians) and two disputed letters (Colossians, 2 Thessalonians). Timothy was Paul's fellow worker travelling with him on his second and third missionary journeys (see Acts 15:1–30; 18:23—21:19). Timothy was no lightweight. He was known among many churches and had an indirect voice in this situation.

Paul greets Philemon, the recipient of the letter, as a "beloved fellow worker." Most scholars take this to mean Philemon was the pastor of this church. Paul also greets Apphia and Archippus who are named as associates with Paul and the church that met in their house. This is another example of Paul making this letter and issue public. Apphia was referred to as a sister, a reference to her being a sister in the Lord. Scholars are not exactly sure what relation she had to Paul, Philemon, and Archippus, but she may have been Philemon's wife and Archippus was their son. The phrase "grace and peace" is Paul's customary salutation and was used in all his letters. The only deviation from the standard grace and peace salutation is found in 1 Tim 1:1 and 2 Tim 1:1, where the word mercy is sandwiched between grace and peace. Grace usually refers to kindness. Mercy is a favor or expression of kindness and goodwill. Peace means harmony or order resulting from being in right relationship with God. All three come from God the Father and the Lord Jesus Christ. Paul's use of grace and peace are different from customary first century letters because of the unique theological meaning inferred by these two words and their relation to the salvific work of Jesus Christ.

THE MASTER'S OTHER SIDE AND THE EXCLUSION OF ONESIMUS: VV. 4–7

Prayers are instructional parts of Pauline letters, revealing aspects of his theology and illuminating issues he would address to the church (e.g., 1 Cor 1:4–7; Phil 1:3, 5; Col 1:3–5, 9). The prayers give clues about the situation at hand—spiritual gifts for the Corinthians, partnership in the gospel in Philippians, and spiritual knowledge and understanding in Colossians. In thanksgiving sections, Paul praises churches, yet also challenges them to grow by using a prayer formula. That is why vv. 4–7 are important in the letter to Philemon. In these verses, clues are given as to the issue Paul is seeking to address in the letter. Paul had been in prayer about this situation and it was no small matter. In his second letter to the Corinthians he mentions the "daily pressure of anxiety for all the churches that he bears." He was a man with deep concern for churches and wrestled with the issues they faced and how best to counsel them. We are invited into this apostolic struggle when we read vv. 4–7 and other thanksgiving sections in his letters.

These prayers also reinforce prayer's role in addressing congregational issues. Paul was a man given to thanksgiving and much prayer for the church. The ministry of prayer was a significant part of the work of first century apostles. In Acts 6, deacons were appointed to free apostles from menial tasks so they would not have to forsake (teaching) the word of God and prayer. In vv. 4–7, Paul is not just greeting these churches and individuals. He is deeply concerned for their spiritual well-being. Because of this, he offers prayers and thanksgiving to God every time he thinks or hears about the people in these churches. Paul's deep pastoral concern and spiritual care for the church sets the tone for the letter to Philemon. An apostle who was deeply concerned for the church was offering counsel seasoned with prayer.

Paul's commendation of Philemon in vv. 4–7 must be interpreted in the larger context of the letter and our under-standing of its occasion. I begin by asking, "What was Paul concerned about in this letter?" On one level, this thanks-giving could appear to commend a Christian pastor for a praiseworthy report. Statements like "I give thanks because I hear of your love and faith" and "I have much joy and com-fort from your love" could appear as a customary greeting filled with compliments and prayers that he might continue doing these things. This is the standard approach of many scholars. But, there is an underlying assumption they use to interpret vv. 4–7, especially scholars who employ the slave flight hypothesis. They believe these statements suggest that Philemon's character is beyond question.[1] John Koenig interprets Paul's commendation as affording to Philemon "high honor," and the reference to "all" in verse 5 "indicates that Philemon has not been prejudicial about his hospitality but has welcomed everyone who comes in the Lord's name."[2] William Barclay boasted that "Philemon was clearly a man from whom it was easy to ask a favor. He was a man whose faith in Christ and love to the brethren was renown, whose story of faithfulness had reached Rome."[3] Koenig went as far as saying, "his house must have been an oasis in a desert."[4] Both statements are exaggerations and examples of assumptions about Paul's intentions. A perspective shift is required. Interpreters have to shift their orientation away from the assumption that Paul was "patting the master on the back for being good." On the contrary, it is worth considering that Paul was actually challenging this pastor and master for not living up to the fullness of his vocation.

Verses 4–5 tell us Paul had heard of Philemon's good works (he had likely heard these things from Onesimus). Paul says that Philemon demonstrated love and faithfulness to all "the saints." Paul also gives thanks for Philemon's faith and love for the saints. These verses suggest that Philemon did things that were good. However, his commendation should not be understood to mean that Philemon was without fault. Philemon had shown the capacity to be

1. Fitzmyer, *Letter to Philemon*, 94; Dunn, *Epistles to the Colossians*, 315–17, 20–21; Lohse, *Colossians and Philemon*, 92–95; Vincent, *Philippians and Philemon*, 177–81.

2. Koenig, *Philemon*, 194.

3. Barclay, "Paul, Philemon, and the Dilemma," 278.

4. Koenig, *Philemon*, 194.

generous toward the saints and that was commendable. It was also strategic and pastoral. Because the letter would be read publicly, it was more helpful to be complimentary and not overtly confrontational like he was in Galatians. Paul's affirmation is a customary practice across his letters yet one can scarcely find a church that perfectly exemplifies love. He did this for pastoral reasons. He uses love as a goal or measure by which to spur the churches toward more mature expressions. I part ways with many exegetes on vv. 4–7. They miss both the subtlety and overall intent of this prayer as an entry point to discussing a problem with Philemon. Paul's commendation was not the result of Philemon's perfect obedience but rather the starting point to a conversation about encouraging and challenging him to grow.

The problem Paul introduces was slowly revealed, beginning with v. 6 when he discusses koinōnia. Why did Paul address koinōnia? Because of Onesimus's experience in the house of his master, Paul uses exclusion to instruct the church about the nature of koinōnia. Though this is considered to be an obscure verse, sounding awkward to the ear, there are three important points that illumine Paul's message and purpose. The first is the translation of the Greek word *koinōnia*, which is often translated as fellowship, participation, or sharing in texts such as 1 Cor 1:9 and 1 John 1:3. With the King James Version, the New American Standard Version, and the American Standard Version, I translate *koinōnia* in v. 6 to mean fellowship. More modern translations such as the New International Version, the New Revised Standard Version, and the English Standard Version prefer the translation rendered "sharing of your faith." While translations may vary, the meaning is clear. Paul is focusing Philemon's attention on what he and Onesimus had in common.

The second significant point is the prayer for Philemon's faith to become active. When Paul prays that the "fellowship of (Philemon's) faith may become effective through the knowledge of every good thing which is in you for Christ's sake," he was mildly critiquing Philemon. Paul prays for Philemon to expand or extend fellowship to house slaves. The implication is clear. Paul is calling out aspects of Philemon's understanding and practice of faith that were ineffectual and needed work. Paul identifies the problem using the language of koinōnia and says in his prayer that Philemon needed "knowledge of every good thing which is in you for Christ's sake."

The third point is the role of knowledge in an effectual or active faith. This point highlights the letter's role in facilitating effectual faith. Once Paul gives Philemon knowledge that fellowship in the gospel should have been extended to house slaves—people he may have viewed as socially inferior to him—the possibility that Philemon might extend fellowship to Onesimus became a reality. What did effectual mean in this verse? I believe it means expanding his circle of fellowship and/or extending fellowship to a slave. This is Paul's prayer for Philemon. Unless Philemon's understanding is changed, he would not be able to extend fellowship to those who were outside his circle of fellowship. The critique here in v. 6 makes his later request in v. 16 possible. Paul emphasizes the role of knowledge because he believes one's capacity for change and newly lived realities are dependent on knowledge, which again, is the occasion for Paul writing this letter. Knowledge activates faith, which changes the dynamics of the relationships between Philemon, Onesimus, and the church that gathered in the house of Apphia and Archippus.

All this, according to Paul, is done for Christ's sake because koinōnia is always both the result of the salvific work of Jesus Christ and the grounds for shared unity in the church. Paul's understanding of koinōnia points to new realities that transform relationships, a belief that radically transcends social boundaries. This is why knowledge is important. Knowledge of what God has done in Christ causes earthly relationships to take on new meaning. Paul wants Philemon to understand this and move from exclusion to inclusion in his fellowship with his slave Onesimus.

On the heels of his first mild critique, Paul softens the tone of the letter by reflecting again on the report he hadsheard. Onesimus's report had not been all bad. Philemon may be a bit duplicitous in his treatment of slaves but he had shown hospitality to others and it was worthy of commendation. Paul was also being strategic and shrewd. In v. 7, Philemon shows he had the capacity for hospitality, refreshing the hearts of the "saints." Paul reminds him how this not only encouraged others but also brought Philemon great joy and comfort, all the more reason for him to offer the same to Onesimus.

PAUL'S APPEAL TO PHILEMON ON BEHALF OF ONESIMUS: VV. 8–9

Verses 8–9 set the tone for the appeal Paul is going to make. Paul models how one who is in authority over others should respond to those under their care. He opens this section with a bold command to do what is right. There are three possible reasons for this bold statement: (1) their personal relationship; (2) his apostolic office; (3) or Philemon's obligation to him for his conversion.[5] The context seems to indicate that Paul is referring to his authority as an apostle. Paul's boldness or authority in Christ allows him to order Philemon to do "what is right" (my translation). The

5. Vincent, *Philippians and Philemon*, 182.

phrase "what is right" is a clear indication that there was something specific Paul had in mind, a standard that was to be upheld in the situation he is addressing with Philemon and this church. In other words, Paul is gently suggesting that there is a right thing to be done. The implication is clear. Paul is throwing his weight around as an apostle and ordering or commanding Philemon, as a pastor, to handle this situation in a certain way. Yet in v. 9, Paul tempers this command with humility, appealing to Philemon in love as "an old man and now prisoner of Christ Jesus."

Paul's appeals to Philemon in love is strategic. Love is a theologically loaded word for Paul and other Christian leaders like the author of John's gospel. Paul is bringing this context to bear on the situation. Agape love is self-giving and ultimately rooted in the example of Jesus Christ who gave himself for others and taught his disciples to do the same. For Paul, this special kind of love is known by the actions it prompts. In Phil 2:1–4 love results in putting others before oneself. In 1 Cor 13:1–13 love that is patient, kind, and unfailing guides the exercise of gifts in the church. In Gal 5:6–15 faith actually works by love. For Paul, love serves as a guiding principle for faith actions and motivates a believer's response to any situation. Paul appeals to love ultimately hoping that Philemon will follow suit.

These verses are important for two reasons. First, Paul's reminder of his apostolic authority puts an incredible amount of pressure on this pastor. This statement holds power and resonates with Philemon and the church. It was as if Paul is saying "I could." One cannot but help wonder if this statement implies he may have done so at a later time because he holds authority over pastors in the churches. The subversive and confrontational nature of the letter is evident here. Second, Paul's refusal to use authority to order Philemon models the kind of response he hopes to inspire.

As the master of his slave Onesimus, Philemon could have punished him for leaving. He could have punished him for reporting the situation to Paul. He had the authority to do so. But was it the right or loving thing to do? That is one lesson Paul tries to teach Philemon.

THE CONVERSION OF A SLAVE WHO WAS FORMERLY USELESS: VV. 10–11

Paul then begins to make his appeal on behalf of Onesimus, Philemon's departed slave, referring to him as his child. He often does this for individuals or congregations he had brought to faith: Timothy in 1 Cor 4:17; Titus in Titus 1:4; the Corinthian Christians in 1 Cor 4:14; and the Galatian Christians in Gal 4:19.[6] The father and child image is sometimes employed in Rabbinic Judaism to describe the relationship between a teacher and a student whom he had instructed in the Torah.[7]

Paul shares what I am certain was an interesting and embarrassing report—Onesimus, who was a non-Christian and a slave in Philemon's household, had become a Christian. For some reason, interpreters miss the significance of this conversion outside the house of Philemon. In fact, they ignore it. For example, Eduard Lohse's commentary in the Hermeneia series ignores this possibility when he comments, "Onesimus had been a slave of a Christian master, but was not yet a member of the Christian community."[8] This fact should not have been so easily overlooked or ignored. It is a significant exegetical issue that Onesimus was not converted under a master known to "refresh the hearts of the saints." Scholars like Lohse and many others fail to

6. Bruce, *Epistles to the Colossians*, 213.

7. Lohse, *Colossians and Philemon*, 200.

8. Ibid., 199.

ask why. Answering this question significantly alters the interpretation of the letter.

Philemon was commended by Paul who prayed that "the fellowship of his faith" would become "effective through knowledge of the good things in us through Christ Jesus." But v. 10 gives us the reason for Paul's prayer. The existence of one unconverted slave in the household, possibly more, has serious implications. Either Philemon and the church did not share their faith or they treated Onesimus in such a way that he was not interested in their faith. In other words, they pushed Onesimus away from faith in Christ. I believe it was the latter. Onesimus could not accept the faith Philemon had modeled in his house, a faith that excluded slaves from fellowship. So when Onesimus left this house, met Paul, and became a Christian, it was an embarrassment to Philemon personally and to that church. It was an indictment of their practice of faith.

There were, however, new possibilities before Philemon and the church once Onesimus had become a Christian. The situation had completely changed. Onesimus was no longer simply an estranged slave of his master. He was now a Christian brother. This meant that Paul's letter must address both the reasons for Onesimus's departure and how Philemon should have responded in light of Onesimus coming to faith. In a sense, Philemon and the church had a second chance to welcome Onesimus, sharing their faith and fellowship in ways that reflected the gospel of Christ Jesus. Paul's careful, heartfelt appeal presents these truths in vv. 11–17. Paul, Philemon, and Onesimus's understanding of the gospel would have everything to do with how the situation is handled.

"Formerly he was useless to you" (v. 11). It is obvious that Paul was using Onesimus's name to make an important point, because his name means "useful," but Paul seemed to be implying something else often missed by exegetes. Traditionally, scholars interpret the verse as Paul using a pun to make a point that a useless slave had become a useful slave once he had become a Christian. Commentators interpret the clause to describe the kind of slave Onesimus used to be before leaving the house and becoming a Christian. Their interpretation is problematic because of the pejorative ways they speak about this slave.

> Onesimus was a "worthless runaway slave."[9]

> Onesimus was "not useful but worthless."[10]

> Onesimus was "a useless slave to his master."[11]

> Onesimus "apparently . . . was useless even before he ran away."[12]

> Onesimus was "useless, not minding his duties, a pilferer and a runaway."[13]

> Onesimus, "I know that you found him the reverse of that . . . quite unprofitable, indeed if not a dead loss."[14]

Scholars have traditionally viewed Paul's "useless" reference through the lens of a culture that sympathizes with the master. The trajectory of thought, which they believe the verse represented, is problematic. Onesimus moves from being a "useless slave" to a "useful slave."

It is obvious that Paul was leveraging his name to make an important point. But what was that point? If new

9. Vincent, *Philippians and Philemon*, 185.

10. Wilson, *Colossians and Philemon*, 350.

11. Lohse, *Colossians and Philemon*, 200.

12. O'Brien, *Colossians and Philemon*, 291–92.

13. Hendriksen, *New Testament Commentary*, 218.

14. Bruce, *Epistles to the Colossians*, 213.

and different questions are being asked, then it is possible to take a fresh look at Paul's purpose. Verse 11 is an integral part of my interpretation because it provides insight into Philemon's thinking about his slave. Philemon's thinking was critical to the experience of exclusion that drove Onesimus away. The phrase "formerly useless to you" is most likely a reference to Philemon's view of Onesimus. Philemon's beliefs about slaves reflected the beliefs of social elites in Colossae and the surrounding region. Slaves were viewed as tools or objects to be used, a belief so pervasive it was even held by philosophers like Aristotle. Considering this church had significant problems with religious syncretism, it is not a stretch to think the syncretism may have also been social (Col 2:8–23).

If Onesimus and other slaves were being excluded and marginalized by first-century Christians, then the phrase that he was "formerly useless" takes on new meaning. Paul could have been suggesting that this was how Philemon viewed Onesimus. Again, commentaries have failed to explore this interpretive possibility. It is possible that Onesimus was useless to Philemon for some reason, such as not diligently working or his consistent failure to complete assigned tasks. It is also possible, and I think quite likely, that "useless" signifies that house slaves were not given the same value as the "saints" (v. 7). In this sense, "useless" was strictly a reference to Philemon's perception of slaves, his low regard for their humanity and worth. Many masters viewed their slaves through a utilitarian lens. A slave's purpose was to perform assigned duties and be socially invisible, and they were purely functional and not invited into relationships, fellowships, or faith communities. This was common cultural practice, and it was likely Philemon both consciously and even unconsciously viewed Onesimus as someone whose worth was directly related to his utility. Because of this, Philemon did not see the need to include Onesimus in his Christian fellowship. Onesimus possibly left Philemon's household because he was treated like chattel. He was "just a slave." While Philemon refreshes the hearts of saints, slaves were treated like property. The cultural context and Paul's phrasing requires the reader to at least consider this as a viable interpretation.

Paul's second phrase that Onesimus was "now . . . useful to me and to you" deserves careful analysis as well. The important word "now" is an indication that Paul was referencing Onesimus's condition as a new Christian. The trajectory of thought in my interpretation is not Onesimus's move from being a "useless slave" to a "useful slave." Rather, Paul states that Onesimus was once viewed by Philemon as "useless" because he was just a slave, but at that point Philemon should have seen him as "useful" because he was a Christian brother and had vocation. Onesimus had a calling to ministry and had proven himself so admirably that Paul wished Onesimus could remain with him (v. 13), but instead Paul sent him back and left it up to Philemon to decide what to do.

There are two thorny issues here. On one level, "useful" referred to Onesimus's utility as a slave to Philemon and a slave of Christ (minister of Paul, vv. 13, 20). Onesimus had returned. Hopefully the letter would dramatically improve the relationship between master and slave. In the end, Philemon would find that Onesimus was useful (meaning different). On another level, the phrase "useful" reflects deeply the value Paul places on Onesimus as a person in vv. 12, 16. Onesimus was not just a slave to be used for tasks. He was a person, a child of God, and a Christian brother to both Paul and Philemon. Onesimus deserves meaningful relationships. Philemon can and should enter into fellowship with Onesimus and grow to love him like Paul had.

Paul confesses his love for Onesimus in v. 12 calling this slave "his heart." There is no escaping the utilitarian dimension of Paul's statement. Paul says Onesimus had value and had a lot to offer Philemon, Paul, and ultimately Christ in service of the gospel. But the gospel changes the meaning of utility as it relates both to masters and the enslaved. Service to God is a Christian virtue and one of the chief aims of any follower of Jesus. Jesus himself taught this before his death in John 13. This makes one's work a part of their service and worship to God, which is different than caring for a master's house. Onesimus now has vocation and is in service to God. Paul is displaying a utilitarian ethic with an egalitarian bend. There were seeds of something radical and genuine in those nine simple words, "now he is useful to me and to you."

While hearing this letter read, Philemon should have been surprised and convicted to hear Paul elevating a slave and conveying such high regard for Onesimus. One who was formerly useless to him had become the "very heart" of the imprisoned apostle. Paul refers to Onesimus in this way to help Philemon make the shift in his own mind and heart and see Onesimus in a new light. Paul also does this to move Philemon from a posture of exclusion to one of inclusion, fully embodying the depth of Christian koinōnia.

ERADICATING "SLAVE STATUS". . . IN THE CHURCH: VV. 15–17

Koinōnia, as radical mutuality, has the potential to undermine inequitable and broken relationships like the one that compelled Onesimus to leave the house of his master. Something new is possible between Philemon, Onesimus, and the church. "Through knowledge of every good thing which is in you" (v. 6), Philemon could extend koinōnia to his departed slave. Here is the knowledge Paul shares. Paul challenges Philemon and the church to a kind of fellowship that had been previously unavailable to Onesimus in v. 6. This exclusion prevents Onesimus from coming to faith in his Christian master's house (v. 10). Paul models the proper use of authority in love in vv. 8–9. He exposes the error in thinking of Onesimus as "useless" when he was in fact useful to Christ and himself in vv. 11–13. Paul even hints that there was a larger purpose for the separation in v. 15. Paul encourages Philemon to welcome Onesimus back in a very different manner than the way he was treated prior to his departure.

Paul makes a radical suggestion that Philemon receive Onesimus "no longer as just a slave, but more than a slave, a beloved brother as a person and in the Lord." Here Paul re-inforces v. 11 and reveals that the problem was perceptional in nature. In v. 11, Onesimus is referred to as "useless," a reference to Philemon's perception of him. The term "useless" is echoed in the phrase "as just a slave" (v. 16). This belief fuels the exclusion Onesimus endured, and is what Paul is challenging and trying to change in Philemon. Commentators Barth and Blanke agree:

> Seen before Onesimus's meeting with Paul and his becoming a Christian—through the eyes of Philemon, of the church members meeting in the Colossian house, and of the Jewish and other non-Christian neighbors, that man had been and still was nothing but a slave—certainly not a brother to his master. As a slave, he was despised rather than loved. . . . For all who spoke about him and had to do with him, including fellow slaves, he was "just a slave" and nothing more.[15]

15. Barth and Blanke, *Letter to Philemon*, 418.

When one is just a slave, or worse yet, chattel in the social structure, it is not a stretch to conclude they experience exclusion. James Dunn is correct that Paul is making a plea for a transformed relationship between master and slave, [16]but it is not because of their shared faith. Rather, it would happen as Philemon is transformed by the renewing of his mind. This is the only way to counter conformity to the world (Rom 12:1–2).

The translation of the first clause is an important interpretive issue. I contend the paraphrase, "no longer as just a slave," over a literal translation, "no longer as a slave," because it more accurately reflects Paul's intent. Commentators like Barth and Blanke and translations such as the TEV and Phillips translate similarly: "no longer as if he were just a slave," "no longer as just a slave," and "not merely as a slave."[17]

The next clause supports this translation by lessening the emphasis to Onesimus's identity as a slave. The phrase "more than a slave," implies "one who is more than a slave—over and above, and designates that which excels or surpasses."[18] The point is that Onesimus could not return to Philemon's house and be viewed as before, with little value, worth, or dignity ascribed to him. Philemon needs to understand Onesimus as more than a slave.

Despite the lack of evidence, some scholars believe Paul is suggesting that Philemon forgive Onesimus for running away. Others argue that Paul is making a veiled request for manumission. Philemon is being asked to transform his way of thinking and behavior. Also, manumission is not the issue in v. 16. On this point, I agree with Craig De Vos. Paul is trying to change the fundamental nature

16. See Dunn, *The Epistles to the Colossians and to Philemon*.
17. Barth and Blanke, *Letter to Philemon*, 417.
18. Blass and Debrunner, *Greek Grammar*, 121.

of their relationship as master and slave, without which, manumission would not make a difference.[19] Paul's concern is not simply that Onesimus is welcomed back in a new and different capacity as a beloved brother and no longer in the capacity as just a slave. His requirement of Philemon goes even further.

Paul calls on Philemon to treat Onesimus as more than a slave. This could suggest Onesimus would remain a slave, at least for that time. Paul is saying, in effect, that Philemon's relationship with Onesimus can no longer be dictated by a legal relationship (master-slave) but by a spiritual relationship (brothers). The NLT captures the sense very well: "He is no longer like a slave to you." At this point, then, Paul is concerned with how the returning slave Onesimus should be viewed by his master.[20]

Moo and others focus on the perceptional change Paul is calling for in v. 16. The perceptional change opens possibilities for Philemon to love Onesimus as a beloved brother on two levels or in two ways—as a person and in the Lord. It would be profound enough for Paul to instruct Philemon to treat Onesimus like a Christian brother. But Paul pushes even further than this, which is why the last phrase, "as a person and in the Lord," is very important. For Paul, kindness and good deeds should always be shared with fellow believers and people in general (Gal 6:10: "do good to all people especially those of the household of faith"). Christians are not called to share good things with only fellow believers. Christians are called to extend them to all persons. Paul teaches this reflects God's universal love, and, more importantly, it has an evangelistic effect, drawing people to Christ Jesus (1 Cor. 9:22–23 "all things to all people that…I might save some").

19. De Vos, "Once a Slave, Always a Slave," 102.
20. Moo, *Letters to the Colossians*, 422.

Two points are in order. First, Philemon did not understand or practice this because Onesimus was not a Christian in his household. Philemon did not connect with Onesimus on a human level, as a brother. This was one reason he was unsuccessful in bringing Onesimus to faith, something that Paul did. Second, slavery dehumanizes people. It objectifies them as chattel, as human tools. Orlando Patterson's work on slavery is helpful. He defines slavery as "the permanent, violent domination of natally alienated and generally dishonored persons" and that in every era it participates in violence, humiliation, and control.[21] Enslaved persons lose their humanity and become tools in households of their masters. Paul is not only saying to treat Onesimus like a Christian brother, which was important. He was also saying, "See Onesimus as a person first." This is qualitatively different than merely allowing him to return without punishment and conferring the title of brother on him. Paul is challenging the core beliefs and culturally normative behavior of Philemon (and this church).

Paul wants Onesimus to be included in the "fellowship of faith" (v. 6) and to share in all the good things that Christ has made available to all persons. Onesimus is not only to be received and welcomed; he is to be given a new status in the church. J. B. Lightfoot's commentary suggests, "The 'no more as a slave' is an absolute fact, whether Philemon chooses to recognize it or not," implying "the termination of Onesimus's former status."[22] This is why I argue that Paul is calling the church to eradicate the "status" of slave in their church. This is the most radical statement in the letter and is extremely difficult to put into practice. Paul does not condemn the institution of slavery. In one statement Paul shows how radical the gospel can be and yet how it

21. Patterson, *Slavery and Social Death*, 13.
22. Lightfoot, *Colossians and Philemon*, 139.

can accommodate itself to culture. He does not take on the institution of slavery here but he does call the church to transform how they relate to one another within the world. Paul did this for theological reasons. Relationships in Christ transcend social distinctions, even if they are not abolished in the social world Christians occupy.[23] Mary Ann Getty explains how the radical elements of the gospel undermine unjust systems like slavery.

> Within the Christian context, Christians can relinquish their survival mentality and together set an example potent enough to convert others with its beauty. Previously, the master/slave, debtor/creditor categories made sense. Since Paul and Philemon and Onesimus have all been baptized, the triangle of mutual obligation is both completed and rendered obsolete. By the same truth that Paul renounces (appealing to Philemon from his position of power), Paul expects Philemon to renounce mastery over Onesimus. Their example brings out the power of the gospel to transform society. Sabotaging what is unjust about human relationships from within, the gospel shows that freedom cannot be imposed, and it also cannot be silenced. The gospel effects a revolution from within.[24]

Getty's recognition that first-century Christians were minorities and adopted a survivalist or accommodationist approach is a compelling argument. New Testament letters encourage civil obedience and cooperation with human institutions like slavery (see Rom 13:1–7; 1 Pet 2:13–17). The household codes reflect this accommodationist perspective (Eph 5:22—26:9; Col 3:18—4:1; 1 Pet 2:13—3:7). But there

23. Dunn, *Epistles to the Colossians and to Philemon*, 334.
24. Getty, "Letter to Philemon," 142.

is a radical element to the gospel in places like Galatians and Philemon. For Paul, Onesimus may legally have been a slave to Philemon but he had as much value, worth, and use as a free person or even a master, and he should have been treated as such. Vincent's comment on this verse captures the power of Paul's request: "Whether Onesimus shall remain a slave or not, he will no longer be regarded as a slave but a beloved brother."[25] Paul's bold request connects with his prayer in v. 6 that Philemon's capacity for koinōnia expand to include one formerly thought of as a useless slave.

Paul makes a radical claim by instructing Philemon not to view Onesimus as a slave but a brother. From v. 8, Paul has been encouraging, even modeling to Philemon how to respond to a situation that is very personal. Paul has repeatedly referenced doing the right thing. So, what is the right thing? The right thing in this context is the eradication of the status of slave, leading to inclusion of all people—even slaves!—in church fellowship. This eradication is possible because of the transformative power of the gospel. Giving all persons, regardless of social or cultural status, a new and equal status in the church is an idea communicated to the church at Galatia and Corinth. Galatians 3:28 levels ethnic, gender, and social status in Christ, while 2 Cor 5:16–17 removes worldly distinctions among Christians. In Christ, all participate in the new creation as children of God. Paul was not only drawing on Jewish and Greek ideas, but he was also drawing upon the revelatory truths given to him by God to speak to Christian slaves.

Paul continues to specify how he wants Philemon and the church to receive Onesimus. He writes, "If you regard me as a partner, accept him as you would me." There is a noticeable shift in tone. For one, Paul speaks more forcefully in the subsequent four verses. This is the first of four

25. Vincent, *Philippians and Philemon*, 189.

imperative statements Paul makes (vv. 18, 20, 22). He also revisits the concept of sharing, partnering, and fellowship. The word "partner" has the same root as "fellowship" in v. 6, and means, "One who shares common interests or who, as comrades, are engaged in the same endeavors."[26] Being a partner implies having common interests, feelings, and work. Though Paul speaks forcefully, he does it using conditional or contingent language, softening the force of his appeal. Conditional statements are assumed true for the sake of argument. Paul is saying, "Let us assume that you regard me as a partner. What would you do for me? You would receive Onesimus as you would receive me."

This bold statement carries as much weight as the preceding verse where Paul challenges Philemon and the church to eradicate the status of slaves in the church. De Vos argues the language of partners was drawn from the domain of hospitality, where receiving a guest meant that the one received became a friend.[27] Dunn argues that "partner" was a commercial metaphor in which Paul was asking Philemon not to punish Onesimus but instead to receive him into his house as he would his partner Paul.[28] While I disagree with Dunn on the idea of foregoing punishment, I do agree on the latter point. Paul wants Philemon to welcome his slave Onesimus as he would receive him, a respected and beloved apostle. Paul wants Philemon to extend to Onesimus the same respect, love, concern, and courtesies that Philemon already shares with Paul.

Paul shows just how much more than a slave Onesimus truly is by requesting that he receive the same treatment. In order to help Philemon shift his thinking so significantly, Paul leverages the goodwill he has with him as an apostle

26. Lohse, *Colossians and Philemon*, 203.

27. De Vos, "Once a Slave, Always a Slave," 103.

28. Dunn, *Epistles to the Colossians and to Philemon*, 338.

and friend, and entreats him to extend it to Onesimus. Clarice Martin suggests the use of partner "serves to illicit loyalty and goodwill, and provides a motive for Philemon to respond."[29] By leveraging goodwill, Paul makes it incredibly difficult for Philemon to deny his request. Paul's invocation of partnership in v. 17 creates anticipation, which is a rhetorical strategy that anticipates the objections before they are given and moves to rectify them or set them aside. Before Philemon could imagine objections to his request in v. 16 (welcome as a beloved brother as a person and in the Lord), Paul adds another layer by commanding Philemon to receive Onesimus as if he were the beloved apostle himself, a fellow partner in the gospel. In fact, Paul expresses confidence in the coming verses, reflecting his anticipation of Philemon's obedience. But before doing this, he addresses a significant matter related to Onesimus's departure.

PAUL'S CONFIDENCE IN PHILEMON'S OBEDIENCE AND PLAN TO VISIT: VV. 18–25

Verses 18–19 seem to indicate that Onesimus may have taken some money from Philemon before leaving and so Paul offers to pay him back. The text does not explicitly state that this happened but many scholars suggest it because Paul is so careful ("if he wronged you or owes you anything"). These scholars conclude Paul uses conditional language because he suspects that either Onesimus did steal from Philemon or that others in the church believed this was what happened.[30] A few go too far in their insistence that the slave had wronged his master and reflect aspects of what we might call "slave master" theology.

29. Martin, "Commercial Language," 329.

30. Fitzmyer, *Letter to Philemon*, 117; Hendriksen, *New Testament Commentary*, 222.

> It is also clear that Onesimus had wronged his master in some way. . . . Since a slave had no legal rights, any matter in which Onesimus denied Philemon his rights to use Onesimus's energies could be regarded as Onesimus acting unjustly toward Philemon. He was also financially in debt to Philemon, which most likely indicates robbery or embezzlement of funds entrusted to him. It should also be recalled, however, that Onesimus's physical removal of himself from Philemon's household would itself constitute an act of robbery, since as a slave, he was technically Philemon's property and since purchase of a slave could be a substantial investment.[31]

This line of thinking is deeply problematic in the matter-of-fact way it speaks about the master having rights to his slave, as if it was a just arrangement. Dunn assumes that the slave was in the wrong for his or her inability to act justly within a system of exploitation, and thus he takes a strictly economic approach to a religious and ethical issue.

It is possible that Onesimus did steal enough money to leave since slaves usually did not have discretionary money to travel. Slavery was a labor and economic institution intended to profit the master by exploiting slaves. It was an institution meant to keep slaves financially dependent on masters who were not always just and equitable in remuneration for their labor. Onesimus may have used Philemon's money to get to Paul, but that is not entirely problematic. Yes, Paul is addressing the last obstacle that may have prevented reconciliation, but he is not doing it in a way that highlights or condemns Onesimus's actions. If Onesimus did steal money, he should not have been harshly judged because he was a slave within a larger system that

31. Dunn, *Epistles to the Colossians and to Philemon*, 302–3

raises deeper questions about just labor, remuneration, punishment, etc.

Two additional points of consideration need mentioning. First, given the possibility that Onesimus was excluded from the fellowship of faith by Philemon and departed the house under the threat of punishment, his departure was most likely rushed. Punishment of house slaves often included severe beatings. Many slaves would flee households because of the threat of beatings. It is possible Onesimus intentionally sought out Paul for intercession in such a matter and needed to get to Paul by any means necessary. Second, and more importantly, it is not necessary to view Onesimus having wronged Philemon by leaving and finding Paul. Actions within unjust and inequitable social systems cannot be measured in the same ethical light as actions emanating from one not in such a situation. It is disappointing that so many New Testament scholars fail to nuance this issue in light of centuries of colonialism, slavery, and racism. Escaping a dehumanizing and marginalizing system and institution is not a horrible wrong. It is reasonable to understand both why Onesimus departed and why he may have taken money to facilitate the journey to the one who could intercede on his behalf.

Another way to view the situation is to understand Paul referring to lost wages that Philemon incurred due to Onesimus's departure. Some scholars concede this possibility. Barth and Blanke rightly add that the statement in question is not a euphemism for stealing.[32] Since a slave was considered the property of the master, the departure of Onesimus inevitably would have caused Philemon financial loss. It is quite possible that Paul is referring to that loss, not theft. That said, it is still necessary to acknowledge the consequences of Onesimus's departure for Philemon, whether

32. Barth and Blanke, *Letter to Philemon*, 481.

there was theft to facilitate the journey to a mediator or loss of wages due to Onesimus's absence. I argue Paul is referring to a situation such as this when he asks if Onesimus "wronged you or owes you anything." Paul is addressing the losses Philemon may have had as a result of his slave's departure. Onesimus is working alongside Paul in prison, and so in the spirit of partnership, he offers to pay Philemon for his losses and for the labor Onesimus offered Paul (v. 13).

Fellowship cannot happen until wrongs are acknowledged and addressed. Paul brings the wrong to light in a sensible manner without humiliating either Philemon or Onesimus. He acknowledges a wrong and moves toward restoration. He neither ignores the wrong nor dwells on it. Paul takes the responsibility on himself for both the wrong done and what is owed. He assumes Onesimus's debt and asks that he be welcomed as if he were Paul himself (v. 17). Inclusive Christian koinōnia places everyone on the same level and requires reciprocal love, respect, kindness, and forgiveness. This properly situates the grounds for restitution Paul outlines. Paul wants to assure Philemon that he would repay him.

Paul also authenticates the authorship of the letter by writing this section of the letter with his own hand. Paul usually dictates his letter or had an amanuensis pen his letters. Both here and in Galatians, Paul mentions he writes with his own hand. This added personal touch gives more credibility and authority to the issue.

Paul makes an interesting comment of personal significance—"not to mention that you owe me your very life." Here, the orator seemingly breezes over something very important to our understanding of Paul's words to Philemon. Paul is shrewd in making such a rhetorical statement that carries a complexity of meaning and incredible weight for his request to Philemon.[33] Paul is likely referring to the fact that he was instrumental in Philemon's conversion. He was either directly or indirectly responsible for Philemon's spiritual life in Christ. Paul makes this statement not to minimize the amount owed to Philemon for lost labor, but rather to demonstrate how Paul handles debts. Philemon is never asked to pay Paul for the riches of salvation that he has experienced. This verse drips with irony and is the second time Paul models for Philemon how the concept of debt works to Christians, in light of Christ.

As Paul moves to conclude his letter, he makes a veiled request of Philemon ("I want some benefit from you . . . refresh my heart"). Paul begins with a bit of a wordplay on the name of Onesimus ("useful"). After promising to repay any wrong or debt owed Philemon, Paul makes a personal request of him. Paul asks to receive a "benefit" for himself, a benefit that closely resembles Onesimus's name. This could be a veiled request: "let me have Onesimus" for myself. Paul, using the optative mode, expresses his desire for Philemon to refresh Paul's spirit. It is quite possible Paul wants Philemon to allow Onesimus to return him and resume his ministry with Paul. In fact, this is the closest Paul gets to making a request for Onesimus to be manumitted.

In vv. 17–18, Paul uses imperatives, but then shifts from being forceful to not wanting to impose his authority as an apostle. In v. 7 Pauls mentions Philemon's reputation of refreshing the hearts of the saints. Now he could refresh the heart of Paul. Again, here is Paul drawing on capacities Philemon had already demonstrated.

Whatever Philemon decides to do with Onesimus would have implications for his relationship with Paul because Paul wants the fellowship they share to be given to Onesimus. This benefit or favor is not entirely personal but

33. Blass and Debrunner, *Greek Grammar*, 262.

is rooted in the gospel. Paul uses "in the Lord" in this verse, implying Philemon's response needs to be first and foremost consistent with the gospel. In the deepest sense, by evoking the realm of the gospel in the situation, Paul hopes Philemon's response will be centered on Christ rather than his own personal desire.

An important ancillary issue is the ministry potential that Paul discovers in Onesimus. Onesimus has been proven to be quite useful and Paul's recognition of his potential for ministry is why he is requesting Philemon refresh his heart. Onesimus is not just a slave but is a fellow believer and an effective fellow worker in the gospel. Philemon could expand what he already did for other believers by sending Onesimus back to Paul to continue his ministry.

Paul is confident that Philemon will obey not only Paul's desire but exceed his expectations (v. 22). His confidence is rooted in two things: Philemon's reputation and the expectation that God would work in the situation. Philemon has a good reputation in the church and ministers out of love and sincerity (vv. 4–7). His love for the saints also gives Paul confidence that reconciliation would occur. Paul expects the Spirit to work in the situation by opening Philemon's heart to love and to welcome all people—not just his peers, but also his slaves and most especially Onesimus.

Since the letter would have been read in the church, Paul places all of the members of Philemon's faith community on notice that he plans to visit them upon his release from prison. This, of course, would give Paul the opportunity to witness firsthand how Philemon and the church reacted to his letter and its plea on Onesimus's behalf. Paul is not only hopeful that he would get out of prison, but he is also hopeful that when he returns to the Lychus River valley he will find his letter has helped reconcile a potentially difficult situation.

Paul concludes the letter by greeting his associates in ministry—Epaphras, Mark, Aristarchus, Demas, and Luke. He offers a final wish that the grace of God be with them.

SUMMARY AND RELEVANCE

In the exclusionary koinōnia interpretation, the departure of Onesimus, his conversion through the ministry of Paul, Paul's assertion that Onesimus was "useless," and his encouragement to receive Onesimus as "not just a slave but a beloved brother as a person and in the Lord" all seem to indicate that exclusion and koinōnia were the letter's central issues. Paul's purpose is to address Philemon's understanding of koinōnia and its bearing on the story of Onesimus. Onesimus was not a Christian in Philemon's house because of the duplicity of his master, who was welcoming social peers while mistreating his household slaves. Paul calls on Philemon to change his way of thinking and to receive Onesimus back as a brother, one with whom he is equal in Christ and with whom he could share Christian fellowship. Paul ends the letter confident that Philemon would make a change in his perspective regarding Onesimus and more. To my mind this is a different, more hopeful, and more redemptive way for the church to reflect theologically on the letter to Philemon than the traditional slave flight interpretation.

QUESTIONS FOR REFLECTION

1. Why did Paul tell Philemon that Onesimus was formerly "useless to him" in verse 11? Why is it important to their relationship as new "brothers" in Christ that Philemon recognize his previous sinful perception of Onesimus?

2. What is unusual about Paul's request that Philemon receive Onesimus back "no longer as a slave but more than a slave, as a beloved brother" in verse 16? Give a modern example of a Christian leader being asked to do a similar thing.

Chapter 4

Theology and the Letter to Philemon

THE LETTER TO PHILEMON is often ignored by the church and believed to lack a theological message. Marion Soards's work on Philemon shows the prevailing belief is that Philemon has little theological substance.[1] Contemporary commentaries are littered with comments that either Philemon does not contain theological material or preoccupy readers with exegetical minutiae. They give only a passing reference to theological matters and questions. For example, Joseph Fitzmyer's excellent commentary on Philemon in the Anchor Bible Series devotes 122 pages to exegetical matters and only four to theological ones. When discussing theology in Philemon, a lot of time is spent chronicling what theological issues the letter does not address—the effects of the Christ event, human sin or any pardon of it, justification by grace through faith, baptism, etc. Fitzmyer details how many times God (2x), Christ (8x), the Holy Spirit (0x) are mentioned in the letter and what it suggests about Paul's

1. Soards, "Some Neglected Theological Dimensions," 209.

theological understanding but not much else.[2] Douglas Moo's commentary in the Pillar series contains no explicit theological discussion of the letter. Instead, Moo focuses on the letter's purpose.[3] In this section, he takes up theological issues, especially the issue of slavery. The problem is that it gives readers the impression that the letter lacks theological substance and, as a result, theological relevance. One of the reasons the letter is believed to lack relevance is methodological. Scholars need a different approach to discerning and utilizing the theological message of the letter to Philemon.

Often scholars focus on exegetical markers, key words or phrases in the text that reflect the theological vision of Paul; familial language, the transcendent nature of relationships in Christ, and reconciliation are just a few example of themes mined by scholars. Some scholars also have addressed the issue of slavery and its relation to Paul's theology of the church, which in the end limited his ability to significantly address the greater evil of slavery itself. Because his focus was on our relationships in Christ over and above worldly relationships, he did not offer a sweeping condemnation of social evils like slavery. Often scholars employ this logic to answer the question of why Paul did not condemn the practice of slavery in Philemon. They argue that what he did in the letter was actually more important and profound than challenging slavery. While helpful, this approach to theology does not go far enough in making relevant connections to modern theological movements and issues.

---

2. Fitzmyer, *Letter to Philemon*, 37–40.

3. Moo, *Letters to the Colossians*, 369–78.

A MESSAGE THE CHURCH CAN NO LONGER IGNORE

The relative lack of interest in Philemon is not only a problem because it is further proof of the decline in reading the full canon of Scripture, but it is a deeper signal that the letter lacks relevance for the church. It is becoming increasingly apparent that Philemon, and I would add its interpretation, have failed to capture the church's imagination. I hope my work on this small letter encourages teachers and preachers to engage the letter for the first time or to reengage the letter from a different hermeneutical standpoint. The departure of Onesimus, his conversion through the ministry of Paul, and the letter that Onesimus brought back to Philemon all indicate that exclusion and koinōnia were the central issues. Because of this, I interpret Paul's commendation to Philemon as addressing his understanding and practice of koinōnia. Onesimus was not a Christian in Philemon's house because of the duplicity of his master, who welcomed social peers and mistreated slaves. There is evidence of this in vv. 10–11. Both the fact that Onesimus was not converted while a slave in Philemon's household and Paul's pun of "useless" seem to indicate that Philemon excluded and marginalized Onesimus due to his enslaved status. Paul calls on Philemon to change his way of thinking and to receive Onesimus back as a brother, as one who is equal with him in Christ and one with whom he shares Christian fellowship. Paul ends the letter confident that Philemon will do that and more. Paul's letter to Philemon still speaks to current theological issues in profound ways when read through the lens of exclusion. It can even speak a word of meaning, hope, and healing to this nation as it continues to grapple with a constellation of issues around faith, inclusion, justice, and relationships.

While I hope readers will find my interpretation helpful and consistent with the text, my primary concern is not my interpretation but encouraging people to engage with the letter more deeply than we are seeing today. I have given exegetical and historical reasons to reengage the letter to Philemon. In what follows, I want to explore the letter for its theology and relevance for the modern church. Drawing on specific verses in the text and its back story, I will consider theological discussions dealing with the practice of faith, evangelism, social advocacy, cultural accommodationism, and modern slavery. When considering American churches and their mammoth struggle with issues of racism, classism, multiculturalism, and economic justice, the letter to Philemon is a book in the Bible that the church cannot afford to ignore any longer. Onesimus is not the only one to run away from a poor witness of the faith. In fact, some of the reasons for declining congregations and the lack of relevance today are due to the church's inability to give witness to a gospel that arrests the attention and energies of religious people. Religious leaders and congregations are alarmed by the steady decline in church attendance. George Barna and David Kinnaman state, "On any given Sunday, the vast majority of Americans are absent from church." They provide compelling data. While 49 percent of Americans can be categorized as actively churched, meaning they attend church at least once a month, 51 percent do not attend. In fact, 8 percent are minimally churched, meaning they attend church infrequently and unpredictably; 33 percent are de-churched, meaning they once were active in church but no longer attend; and 10 percent are purely unchurched, meaning they do not currently and have never attended a church.[4] What is even more disturbing is that, as the American population continues to grow, the number

4. Barna and Kinnaman, *Churchless*, 6.

of people attending churches continues to decrease, and if these trends continue, by 2050 the percentage of Americans attending church will be half the 1990 figure of 52 million.[5] That would mean that only 27 million Americans will attend church (population estimates in 2015 are over 430 million). These statistics overlook the people who are not going to a Christian church because they are attending other religious services—temples, mosques, synagogues. The United States is more diverse than it was in the early nineties. This, too, is part of the story behind these percentages but does not take away from the larger truth that people are leaving the church en masse. Studies are showing that a growing number of Americans are turned off by religion, and worse yet, many Christians are turned off by the very churches they once attended.

There is more to this decline than churches not keeping up with things like population growth. Declining congregations are a microcosm of the growing irrelevance of churches in a diverse, socially conscious, and pluralistic society. There is a widening disconnect between churches and people, especially millennials who say they dislike what they see in churches. In a quest to understand the decline of churches, especially the fact that millions of people who claim to be Christian no longer attend church, some leaders have been frank in their assessment that we Christians bear some blame. Pastor John Pavlovitz argues that churches ignore major issues like poverty, racism, and violence. The church's love doesn't look like love but rather like a brand of love that is incredibly selective and decidedly narrow.[6] There are many ways to interpret and elaborate on what Pavlovitz names, but what seems to ring true is that too many churches do not practice what they preach or live

5. Olson, *American Church in Crisis*, 16.
6. Pavlovitz, "Church."

into their calling as disciples of Jesus in a way that connects to people's hearts. Like Onesimus, many people perceive a disconnect between the faith proclaimed and the faith enacted.

I have found in my work on the issue of clergy suicide that other reasons fuel congregational decline—toxic and dysfunctional congregations that have turned people away at the church door.[7] Some congregations are contentious, and worse yet, they don't cultivate the spirituality they preach and sing about every week. For example, the eleven o'clock hour continues to be the most segregated hour or hours of the week even though these people are supposed to be worshipping the same God. Furthermore, Barna found that biweekly attendance at worship services are, by believers' own admissions, generally the only time they worship God. Eight out of every ten Christians surveyed did not feel they had entered the presence of God or experienced a connection with God during the worship service. Half did not feel they had entered the presence of God or experienced a genuine connection with him during the past year.[8] These are but a few examples evidencing the significant decline we are witnessing in the second decade of the twenty-first century. Is it possible that more Americans are leaving churches because they do not see genuine fellowship? Is it possible they are not seeing fellowship because people in church are not experiencing fellowship with God through Jesus Christ and then sharing it with others? They go to church. They sing. They hear sermons. But they are not experiencing the kind of fellowship Paul envisioned in the letter to Philemon.

7. Brogdon, *Dying to Lead*, 28–31.
8. Barna, *Revolution*, 31–32.

THE DEEPENING AND BROADENING OF FAITH

"I pray that the fellowship of your faith may become effective through knowledge of every good thing in us through Christ" (v. 6)

A good place to begin is with Paul's use of fellowship. He challenges the sinful practice of faith that excludes marginalized persons and offers an invitation to drink deeper from the well of faith. Paul prays for Philemon to deepen and broaden his understanding and practice of faith. In a real sense, this is exactly what is ailing American Protestantism. Much of what is practiced in Christian communities, congregations, and homes across the country is good, but in need of deeper and broader manifestations of Christian faith. While good, the shallow nature of Christian witness today—segregated churches by race and class, widespread nominalism, silence about and support of various social injustices—is a serious threat to the Christian faith and part of the reason Christianity is experiencing malaise and decline. In Philemon, Paul hints at what could revitalize the church.

The theological message of the letter to Philemon begins with Paul's understanding of fellowship with God and fellowship with one another. Paul went through the trouble of teaching Philemon and this church the truth, as obscure as v. 6 sounds—(*[I pray] that the fellowship of your faith may become effective through knowledge of every good thing in us through Christ*). Only by fully understanding our deep and reciprocal relation to each other can we deepen how we practice Christian faith in community and the world.

I describe koinōnia as "radical togetherness" that disrupts worldly systems and social relations. The Greek word *koinōnia* can be translated as "fellowship" and also as "participation." Both translations and connotations communicate rich truth about the meaning of faith in Christ and how it was shared with others. Paul commonly uses the term koinōnia in reference to the mutual "fellowship" of believers that resulted in sharing and generosity.[9] *Koinōnia* is multidirectional. It begins with Christ. In 1 Cor 1:9, believers are called to fellowship with the Son, a reference to our spiritual communion with him. Similar to 1 John 1:3, where John invites recipients of his letter to participate in their fellowship and confesses that his fellowship is with the Father and the Son Jesus Christ. *Koinōnia* begins with Christ, but it extends outward to fellow believers and all people. While fellowship was the term often used for koinōnia, it carries other meanings that shed light on how believers related to one another. *Koinōnia* can also mean (1) communion, (2) generosity or fellow-feeding, (3) a gift or contribution, and (4) sharing.[10] The fact that *koinōnia* is linked to communion is significant (1 Cor 10:16ff). Communion is one of the most important Christian sacraments shared by believers, calling us to remember the death of Jesus and to examine how we treat one another as members of Christ's body. *Koinōnia* reflects deep Christian practices like generous giving and sharing what one has with others. Acts 2 and 4 chronicle Christian fellowship and sharing. Both the ordinance of communion and practices like giving and sharing are based on our common faith and participation in the ministry of Jesus, and are, by their nature, radical expressions of togetherness that counter worldly social visions of human relationality.

Koinōnia is a kind of fellowship characterized by a close bond and a two-sided or reciprocal relationship. In other words, Christian fellowship is not merely characterized by

9. Hauck, "Koinōnia," in Kittel, *Theological Dictionary of the New Testament*, 797–809.

10. Arndt and Gingrich, *Greek English Lexicon*, 438–39.

"get-togethers" or when "saints" gather in the building we call a church. What *koinōnia* suggests is that Christian fellowship is rooted in a deep relational and reciprocal bond "in Christ." That is why Paul uses familial language and the metaphor of the church as a body in his letters. He often instructs churches with the language of sisters and brothers, members of one body, and bonded together in Christ.

This theme is central in Philemon. One of the letter's distinguishing features is the abundant use of family language. Words like "brother" in vv. 1, 7, and 20, "sister" in v. 2, "dear friend" in v. 1, "saints" in v. 5, "elder" or "old man" in v. 9, "my son" in v. 10, and "dear brother" in v. 16 inundate the letter. These words communicate the important theological concept that Christians are connected and a part of the spiritual family of God. Paul uses familial language because of his understanding of *koinōnia*.

This word also conveys a deeper truth about the meaning of Christian relations in a sinful and unjust world. Christian "fellowship" suggests that Christian bonds transcend social distinctions. Paul is clearly thinking about the transcendent nature of relationships in Christ in the letter to Philemon. Paul's treatment of both Onesimus and Philemon models this kind of relationship, one that has no regard for social distinctions. Being "in Christ" transforms the nature of social relationships in the church. Since Onesimus was a believer, he should have been received as a brother and not merely a slave.

Koinōnia, however, does not transcend social distinctions in the sense that it sits on top of them and does not change them. Christian fellowship should at best dismantle and at least unravel the fabric of unjust social arrangements. Philemon was called to faithfully treat Onesimus as a brother, not a slave. This distinction is important because often the language of transcendence is used to avoid the social and political implications of faith. Paul does not call for the abolishment of slavery, but he does seem to rebuke Philemon and challenge him and the church to eradicate the slave status in the church. This was a move that could have unraveled the fabric of a society built on slavery. In v. 19 Philemon is reminded that he owes the aged apostle his very life. The blessings Philemon enjoyed are a result of the apostle leading him to Christ. This gives the apostle's request new meaning. Again, this was only understood in the context of the transcendent nature of relationships "in Christ." Paul's focus on the nature of these relationships may have limited his ability to address significantly the greater evil of slavery itself. Because his focus is on our relationships in Christ over and above worldly relationships, he does not offer a sweeping condemnation of social evils like slavery.

Even though *koinōnia* can be translated as fellowship and/or participation, I want to propose some pastoral nuance to the implications of this word for Christian faith. *Koinōnia* as "radical togetherness" cannot be practiced unless one experiences fellowship or participation in the life of Christ. Paul uses the term *koinōnia* thirteen times in his letters to denote the religious fellowship of the believers in Christ. This connotation is why scholars prefer the translation "participation." It means one enters a two-sided relationship with the living Christ. Paul calls it fellowship when one interacts with, learns from, and follows Jesus in a way that transforms their life and their view of the world and value of things.

In Phil 3, Paul considers fellowship with, or participation in, the life of Christ to be the most important and valuable thing. His achievements and worldly accruements pale in comparison to the knowledge of Christ that he gained by participating more deeply in the life of Christ.

He describes his life's quest in this way: "that I may know him, and the power of his resurrection, and the fellowship (participation) of his sufferings, being made conformable to his death" (Phil 3:10). Here Paul talks about *koinōnia* as a real fellowship or participation in the life of Jesus Christ. This pastor of twenty-five years understands that one's personal, spiritual, and active relationship with Christ or lack thereof significantly influences the living out of one's faith. The deeper the level of participation in the life of Christ—prayer and worship that commune with God, meditation on Scripture that transforms the mind, and confession of sin that purifies the heart—the deeper and broader one's practice of faith will become. In the absence of such participation, one's practice of faith will remain shallow and exclusive. There is a real need today to reemphasize practices related to Christian piety and spirituality, because without real communion with God, Christians are unable to grasp and live out what it means to follow Jesus.

Koinōnia as fellowship means that faith is something that broadens over time. *Koinōnia* as participation means that faith is something that deepens as it is rightly understood and exercised. Paul emphasizes these aspects in v. 6, an incredibly instructive verse for the church today. The often shallow and narrow practice of Christian faith has caused millions to repudiate a Christian witness that neglects the poor and continues to marginalize women. To use Paul's language in Romans, it shows that such churches are merely conformed to the world. American congregations need to better understand what this word means and how it can help correct congregational cultures that are mired in evils like racism, classism, and sexism. *Koinōnia* as both the deepening and broadening of faith has a transcendent dimension to it, one that resists cultural accommodation. More importantly, it invites us into the struggle to overcome the central issue and strong temptation of cultural influences. Theological reflection on the letter to Philemon is challenging because there are both radical ("accept him no longer as a slave") and accommodationist ("whom I am sending back to you") elements intertwined in these twenty-five verses. It is critically important to draw on both elements in different ways to benefit from the rich theological material in Philemon.

THE PROBLEM WITH THE CULTURAL ACCOMMODATION OF THE GOSPEL

"He was separated so you might have him back forever. No longer as just a slave but more than a slave, a beloved brother . . . as a person and in the Lord" (vv. 15–16)

Good theology is discerned through the struggles and tensions to be faithful to God in a sinful world. The letter to Philemon is a powerful example of one of the great struggles the church faces in the fight to give witness to a liberating gospel in a world filled with injustice because it deals with the treatment of slaves by Christians. Paul carefully speaks to the issue of exclusion and *koinōnia*, requesting that Philemon discontinue the practice of viewing and treating Onesimus as "just a slave" and instead as a "beloved brother" (v. 16). Yet he neither gives a critique of the institution of slavery in the Greco-Roman world nor problematizes slaveholding for Christians. New Testament scholars offer their explanations for why Paul could not even imagine doing such a thing or why he did not do this in any of his letters.

David Garland's work on Philemon and ancient slavery is one example of this kind of thinking. He provides five differences between ancient and contemporary slavery.

Though his focus is on differences between the two forms of slavery, he illustrates historical links in a way that is helpful in the following discussion. We should not assume that all first-century slaves were poorly treated and desperately wanted to escape slavery. Ancient slavery did not have any racial undertones. Since education enhanced the slave's value to an ancient slave owner, it was encouraged and prized. Since race did not destine one for slavery, most ancient slaves did not think of their slavery as a permanent condition. In contrast with the average inhabitant of Paul's world, the average Southerner had little personal contact with slaves.[11] For these reasons, Garland not only considers the institutions to be different, but also, suggests that one should not fault Paul for his failure to condemn slavery as morally inconsistent with the Christian gospel.

> Today, some consider Paul's inattention to the social inequities of slavery to be a deplorable blind spot, but it may instead be based on his unclouded vision that such things are ultimately meaningless. He was fully aware that the existing social order was deeply flawed (see Rom 1:18–32), but he expected the present scheme of things to pass away soon (1 Cor 7:29–31). . . . The meaning of slavery was therefore transformed. Christians could serve the Lord in whatever situation or station they found themselves in life.[12]

While I appreciate Garland's recognition of the fallen and unjust nature of the world, this line of thinking is problematic. First, the statement that "social inequities of slavery" are "ultimately meaningless" because they are a part of a flawed social order that Paul believes was passing away is a statement lacking both pastoral and theological concerns.

11. Garland, *Colossians and Philemon*, 349–51.
12. Ibid., 340.

As the body of Christ, we are called to care for people and the real-world issues that affect their lives. This care is pastorally based and rooted in a theological belief that goes deeper into the example of God who shows presence and care for the vulnerable. Garland's statement sweeps over many whose lives were affected by slavery. This thinking reveals the deeper theological problem with the slave flight interpretation and the general way interpreters approach Philemon theologically. Much of the theology offered by these interpreters has an accommodationist tint that absolves them from challenging social injustices like slavery.

I approach slavery and the letter to Philemon differently. I believe Paul undermines and subverts aspects of slaveholding by Christians in the letter to Philemon. But I recognize his refusal to give a clear condemnation of it here and in writings such as 1 Corinthians and Colossians opens the door for centuries of ambiguity on the issue. This ambiguity results in later Christian leaders believing that Paul supported slavery (1 Cor 7:21–22; Eph 6:5) and thus feeling less moral pressure to resist slaveholding to order society. This, in the end, leaves them more inclined to suppose divine sanction and defend the institution.

Many scholars are adamant that it is absurd to expect Paul to launch a broader critique of slavery and slaveholding by Christians because "in the ancient world slavery was accepted as an integral part of society and its economic working."[13] The treatment of slaves was the moral question, not slavery itself. Some scholars believe it is also unfair because Paul could not bear the weight of history and had no way of knowing the legacy of slavery in the church. Therefore, Paul, the author of the most writings in the New Testament, could not bear a shred of blame for how later church leaders would use his writings to defend slavery. In

13. Dunn, *Epistles to the Colossians*, 306.

fact, I used to think this way. There was a time I could not imagine criticizing Paul. Take for example what I wrote in the conclusion of my master's thesis.

> After examining Pauline slave texts and reading thousands of pages of research, my conviction that the Bible is the greatest book ever written is not shaken. In the end, the greatest paradox I have encountered was not a paradox because the Bible does not undergird the institution of slavery. Therefore, African-American Christians can look to the Bible and to Paul for a vision of humanity that they can trust. The love and grace of God and how Paul understood God to be at work in humanity was such that it included all—even slaves. Paul's vision was inclusive. African Americans do not have to be suspicious of Paul because his words were spoken to be a blessing to all. Paul was not the cause for the slavery that destroyed millions of African Americans. His words were used in a way that was grossly inconsistent with his theological vision of slavery. If one interprets Paul's references to slaves in the proper theological and cultural context, then the radical nature of the gospel will be very evident. The gospel message proclaimed by Paul to those who were slaves was one of equality before God. That is why I believe that Paul was anti-slavery. Paul understood that before God and in the church, social distinctions carried no weight. A proper interpretation of Paul's writings concerning slavery must include this understanding. If so, then one is not given the latitude that was used in earlier times in America to justify slavery. . . . Paul "Christianizes" slavery in his writings. I hope that my exegesis of Ephesians 6 and Philemon 1:8–16 have thoroughly demonstrated that point. Slaves are moral and ethical agents.

Slaves are both autonomous, being responsible for their lives to God, and a part of Christian community as brothers and sisters. Slaves serve Christ by faithfully performing their tasks. They will be rewarded at the eschaton for the faithful performance of earthly duties to earthly masters. Slaves are valued for the things that they do and loved as children of God. Slaves are to be regarded as dear brothers and sisters. They are family. In fact, they are not to be regarded as slaves in the church.[14]

I thought I had exonerated Paul on this issue and settled a few others until my thesis supervisor Marion Soards wrote this one question in the margin: "Is it so easy?" As a third-year seminary student in my early thirties, I was not ready to critique one of my heroes, one who wrote so many books in the New Testament. My years of training by conservative teachers who believe in the inerrancy and infallibility of the Bible had conditioned me to view Paul himself as infallible and incapable of imperfections and blind spots, as one who in no way had privilege as a free person participating in a system that exploited others. Because of this, I refused to dig deeper into this issue, content on defending Paul and ignoring the valuable lessons that even shortsightedness provided the church. But that simple question stuck with me, because it rings true. It is not so easy to exonerate Paul or any of us for that matter. Our world is too interconnected and interdependent. We need theologies that do not quickly pass over such complex issues.

Should we let Paul or any church leader off the hook? There are three reasons why we, collectively, should not. First, Paul received personal revelations from God and insights into the mysteries of God that went beyond his

14. Brogdon, "Interpreting Pauline Slave Texts," 91–92, 94.

ability to fully understand. He had the potential to envision beyond the immediate time. Second, Paul was very forward thinking and radical about issues of inclusion (Jews and Gentiles, male and female, rich and poor, and slaves and free persons). Third, he was politically savvy, insisting that Christians respect government powers and social order, and yet he disobeyed certain laws and restrictions placed on his ministry and opposed religious establishment and practices that were unjust and antithetical to the gospel. He opposed authority. There is no reason an apostle with his vast knowledge and insight into spiritual matters could not have addressed the issue of slavery in a clear and more forthright manner. I am not condemning Paul nor saying he was a failure but rather showing that this great leader of early Christendom had blind spots and limits that are instructive for the witness of the church today.

Paul's unwillingness to critique slaveholding as antithetical to the gospel provides a powerful example of what happens when the church does not go far enough to help the world envision better ways to live together. The consequences, though unintended and beyond our ability to grasp fully, are very real, deeply painful, and sometimes deadly. And so, this letter and its interpretation are a sober warning against attempts to soften the radical nature of the gospel. An important part of ministry is pushing the bounds of the gospel, preventing culture from domesticating and softening the gospel's edges and grand vision. This is a struggle for both Paul and the church universal.

If we continue the practice of letting Paul off the hook we more than likely will do the same for ourselves and our forebears. We will continually justify why it is acceptable to be a person of our time. I suspect this kind of scholarship is one reason the church closes its eyes to slavery today and the aspects of capitalism that are exploitative, oppressive, and unjust instead of leading the world to envision how we can better order ourselves socially, politically, and religiously. The sad truth is that we cannot imagine a world where such practices are not foundational to the building of a wealthy society. Such lack of vision is partly the church's fault for being the puppet of the state rather than its conscience, as Martin Luther King Jr. taught Christians in America decades ago. And, we're seeing more socially conscious and justice minded Christians leaving churches because of a gospel that is too accommodating to the culture, too likely to send Onesimus back and let Philemon decide what is best.

THE ROLE OF ADVOCACY
IN CHRISTIAN MINISTRY

"I appeal to you concerning my child Onesimus"
(v. 10)

There are three very powerful theological messages in Philemon. First, this letter lays out one way to work toward liberating the world and redemptive ways of living in the world where structural inequities abound. Paul's letter to Philemon provides a rough template of how to work toward the best possible expression of reconciliation amid social arrangements that are structurally unjust. What I mean with the careful language of "the best possible expression of reconciliation" is that there may be situations where it is appropriate to imagine reconciliation. For example, situations with discord and animosity between family members or friends. There are, however, situations where reconciliation is not possible until structural change occurs. I will conclude with an example of the latter.

In Philemon, Paul intercedes between people experiencing estrangement. His position of authority allowed him to speak to Archippus, Apphia, Philemon, and the church in ways Onesimus could not. Paul advocates for Onesimus who was in a socially precarious position as a slave. Paul acts as a social advocate as he dealt with religious, economic, legal, and class issues. Paul advocates for Onesimus and works to bring to fruition the best possible expression of reconciliation, without doing away with the larger system of slavery. The fact that Onesimus left Philemon's house indicates estrangement. As an advocate, Paul facilitates healing for the offenses Onesimus experienced and reconciliation between master and slave. Whether it happened depended on other factors, such as Philemon and the church at Colossae's receptivity to Paul's correction and instruction. It also depended on their willingness to sacrifice privilege and pride to restore right relationship. In this sense, advocacy makes reconciliation possible, not actual, a needed correction to those who are too quick to call for reconciliation when deeper discussions about repentance and privilege have not occurred. When reconciliation is misunderstood, the marginalized continue to bear the scars and are silenced from needed discussions about retribution and justice.

Admittedly, there is some tension in the letter with the issue of privilege. Privilege is an indicator of an inherently unjust situation. The world is structurally unjust because people with power and privilege structure it in ways that reward the few and exploit the many. For Paul, this is ultimately an apocalyptic and eschatological issue (i.e., "present evil age"). Structural justice is the standard and goal that we work toward. This suggests that being faithful means participating or joining with God in manifesting justice in the world. However, the hard truth is that its full manifestation will not come until the Parousia. The work we do with God seeks to dismantle and/or unravel these systems as we give witness to the radical and liberating message of the gospel of Jesus Christ. And so, the important lesson, in a world where there are masters and slaves, free persons and enslaved persons, and religious leaders and religious communities, is how one uses privilege. There is much work that needs to be done on this issue from a biblical standpoint.

Paul's actions teach two important truths about the role of advocacy as it relates to privilege. First, Paul was privileged and is using his privilege. Second, Philemon was also in a place of privilege and needed to be corrected, making a sacrifice or relinquishing his privilege as it related to his slave Onesimus. These two truths raise an important question, "If good persons relinquish privilege (second truth), how can they use it?" The answer is they use it to advocate for those without it (first truth). By advocating for Onesimus, Paul shows that privilege is not something to hold on to or to lord over others but rather something to be used to advocate for others and to give witness to values rooted in the radical mutuality that characterizes Christian fellowship. In this way, the letter to Philemon provides a way to repair some of the fragmentation that results from unjust social structures and norms by dealing with the privilege the system gives some and withholds from others.

Paul's struggle in Philemon is repeated throughout history. It is no small task to live out the radical vision of the kingdom of God in a world structurally opposed to it. But in and through the struggle, Christians have gained wisdom they gratefully shared that can illumine our present struggles to live out the gospel.

Martin Luther King Jr. was a leader who lived the struggle of being an ambassador of Christ working to reconcile people to God. His "Letter from a Birmingham Jail" provides insight into his own experience. The letter was

written in response to white clergy who questioned why
he came to protest in Birmingham, Alabama, causing such
a stir that it landed him in jail. King responded that this
was an injustice. He said, "Injustice anywhere is a threat to
justice everywhere." The Christian expression of deep compassion for others requires risk and leveraging positions of
privilege to fight injustice and prevent injury.

King was a Baptist minister willing to risk what he
had in the struggle for civil and human rights. He did this
because he believed all humans are "caught up in an ines-
capable network of mutuality."[15] This idea is very similar
to Paul's teaching on the body of Christ. We share a deep
mutual connection that should manifest itself in a profound
care for others, especially the socially marginalized. King
showed how to act out that care because, more often than
not, humans are content to express care only verbally. Real
care must be expressed by taking action to alleviate the
suffering that someone else may experience. In particular,
care is demonstrated through direct action and constructive negotiation. The path to resolution is only possible
through direct action (think confrontation). Confrontation
is needed because it creates tension or a crisis. Before clos-
ing the letter, King also expressed his disappointment at the
silence of white ministers and the passive acceptance of a
status quo that refused to challenge injustice. Their silence,
hesitance to get involved, and acceptance of status quo was
not simply a neutral position. It communicated a lack of
compassion, something both Jesus and Paul criticized. For
King, their response was very unchristian. In this famous
African-American epistle, King taught the importance of
care for people experiencing injustice. He called for a willingness to risk (or use) privilege to apply moral pressure on

15. King, "Letter from a Birmingham Jail," in *Testament of Hope*,
290.

others, prioritizing gospel or kingdom norms over worldly ones and applying them to their network of familial and social relationships. On individual, congregational, and social levels, this practice will weaken and undermine the fabric of an unjust society.

I see a connection between what Paul was doing for Onesimus and what King sought to do for African Americans. They were both advocates. While Paul may not have been applying direct action like Martin Luther King Jr., he was speaking up on behalf of Onesimus who was clearly in need of a champion. The actions of both Onesimus and Paul create tension—leaving the house of Philemon, meeting up with Paul, and writing a public letter challenging a master. Paul applies moral pressure on Philemon to respond favorably to his request. In addition, it was commendable that Paul used his apostolic influence to speak for one who did not have a voice. Paul did not side with the privileged, possibly because he was not writing this letter from a place of privilege, being imprisoned himself for the gospel. Paul sided with the slave Onesimus and pled his cause. Paul referred to Onesimus as his very heart, ending his letter with the request for Onesimus to be accepted as a beloved brother in the flesh and in the Lord, no longer as a slave. He promised to repay Philemon for lost revenue because Onesimus was absent, and to follow up on the situation personally. He was an advocate for Onesimus. The church needs more advocates like Paul. In this vein, the letter of Philemon serves as a guide for the churches in our current ministry of advocacy for the Onesimus's of our modern world.

INJUSTICE AND EXCLUSION
IMPEDE CONVERSION

"Onesimus…whom I have begotten in my bonds"
(v. 10)

In the letter to Philemon, Onesimus was not converted until he left the house of his "Christian" master. The significant question of the letter is Why? I believe he was not converted because Philemon treated him as a "useless slave," excluding him from the fellowship he shared with members of the church at Colossae. Onesimus's experience of exclusion and treatment as "just a slave," became an impediment to conversion. The letter to Philemon, therefore, represents Paul's intervention in the matter. In the letter, he prays that Philemon's "fellowship of faith" is broadened to include Onesimus. Paul calls Philemon to reevaluate Onesimus's worth in light of his new Christian faith and his value to the imprisoned apostle. At the exegetical level, we see that Paul addresses the things that kept Onesimus from becoming a Christian in the first place and the thing that may have kept others in Colossae from doing the same. Paul's actions are instructive for congregations today that inadvertently do things that send the wrong message to others about the meaning of Christian faith and practice. Furthermore, his actions challenge dysfunctional congregations that abuse people of faith. Both types of churches damage people, turning them away from the good news of Jesus.

The second theological message deals with evangelism. This letter is a small treatise on evangelism because it shows how a poor Christian witness can sometimes be the thing impeding or preventing people from hearing the good news of Jesus Christ. The story of Onesimus is also the story of the church today and is why this letter is relevant for the church now more than ever. There are many like

Onesimus who are not Christians, not interested in faith because of the witness of Christians (the church) in their relational sphere. Many are uncomfortable with the word "evangelism" and any language about conversion. Sharing one's faith, teaching others about Jesus, and sharing the good news of the gospel is a fundamental aspect of what it means to be a Christian. It was a command given by Jesus before his ascension. In using the word "evangelism," I mean it in the sense of sharing the good news of Jesus and not in converting people. "Evangelism" is giving witness to the good news of Jesus Christ in three ways: (1) teaching people about Jesus, (2) addressing the reasons people do not believe in the gospel, and (3) addressing the obstacles that keep people from believing the good news. The first aspect has a long history in the church and is still practiced today, even though there is serious decline. The latter two aspects of evangelism have rich applications for our understanding of its practice. For example, it would mean the church is called to address not only philosophical objections to Christian faith, like the problem of evil or agnosticism, but also social justice issues in the world, like poverty, slavery, and sexism, all of which can impede the way to faith. The letter to Philemon is instrcutive on this different way of thinking about evangelistic work. The church is not called to save the world but rather to give witness to the gospel. God saves people, but it is our calling to be faithful to the content of our proclamation and the context of the message. We must learn how to apply the gospel amidst the various philosophical, political, religious, and social challenges of the world and to care for the world effectively. The letter challenges the church to care about Onesimus and people like him because human compassion is a critical component to evangelistic work. Compassion and evangelism should go hand in hand. Compassion should cause us to learn how the systems in the world work—how things like poverty, environmental problems, economic inequalities, violence, and educational disparities shut the door of the gospel. We should learn about these things because they cause intense suffering for many people. Sadly, in learning such things, we are forced to face the diverse ways Christians and sometimes churches support these damaging issues. In addition to the message to Philemon, we ought also to remember Jesus' sober warning about offending little ones in Matt 18. Turning Onesimus and the little children away from him is a serious offense.

There is an undercurrent of hope in this letter. On one hand, it is a painful reminder of the tumultuous history of evangelism. Onesimus was turned off by the witness of faith in Philemon and did not come to faith in his house church in Colossae. On the other hand, it shows us the mystery of evangelism. Onesimus journeyed to Rome (or Ephesus) to see Paul and encountered a different and more inclusive witness of Christian faith. In prison, Onesimus experienced liberation and became a Christian. In the Black church, we call it the "but God" moment because it points to the powerful and pervasive ways God brings hope out of despairing situations. Onesimus could have spent the rest of his life without knowing God's love in Jesus Christ if it was up to Philemon, but God had someone else.

This story resembles the story of many others, including women and minorities, who come to faith in obscure places and less than ideal circumstances despite the ways Christians in their relational sphere misrepresent the gospel. This highlights the mysterious dimension of conversion, despite the church's failing always to embody faithfully the good news. When I teach courses on the history of the Black church, I am reminded of this mystery because so many Africans in America came to faith in

Jesus, even though the practice of Christianity was grossly misrepresented by so many white Christians and in their churches. It is an absolute miracle how they took aspects of what they encountered, noticed the few whites who were faithful to the gospel, and added it to what they were experiencing from the God who met them in the bushes to create a tradition that more faithfully gave witness to the gospel. The birth of the Black church during slavery was a miracle! I marvel at God's power every time I think about it because widespread rejection of Christianity could have been a reasonable response. In some ways, the same thing is happening today. Many people are coming to faith despite us. It is miraculous that so many people believe in Jesus today despite the ways many Christians model the gospel. There is a brand of the gospel that leaves most of the world's population mired in poverty and victims of exploitative and greedy millionaires and billionaires, many who claim to be Christians. In the end, reading Philemon should elicit praise to God, who finds creative ways through the Holy Spirit to use imperfect people and circumstances. It should challenge us to represent more faithfully this message no matter where we are—from prisons to palaces.

THE REVITALIZATION OF THE CHURCH

"Onesimus . . . was formerly useless to you but now he is useful to me and to you, whom I am sending back to you, that is, my very heart" (vv. 11–12)

The exclusionary koinōnia interpretation is an exciting approach because it provides a third theological word that is challenging, yet hopeful, to churches that are declining in America but exploding in the Global South. The hope deeply ingrained in the letter to Philemon can be found in the act, the one so controversial with the slave flight interpretation. Paul sent Onesimus back to Philemon and the church. In the exclusionary koinōnia interpretation, this was an act of providence aimed to revitalize Philemon and the church. In a sense, Onesimus was like a missionary sent by God with a letter to help his new brothers and sisters gain a deeper understanding of the fellowship of faith. However, this could only happen if the church and Philemon embraced the challenge and changed how they viewed Onesimus and other house slaves. Philemon thought his slave was useless (v. 11), but God and Paul thought differently. Onesimus was a beloved child of God and had gifts for ministry ("he is useful to me"). Paul sent Onesimus back, not just because he was legally bound to return a slave to his master, but more importantly, because God wanted to transform a church. Onesimus's return required the church at Colossae to change because God was at work renewing her. There was a seed of congregational renewal and revitalization in the letter to Philemon that is instructive for the church today. The third theological message in Philemon is that the revitalization of our churches will happen when we change our perspective on people we consider minorities and outsiders, release them from conditions of perceptional inferiority, and send them back to our churches that so desperately need renewal. The letter teaches that we are not able to reach the Onesimus's of the world and church with the gospel until we see them differently. There is an inextricable link between the renewal of the church and the renewal of the mind (see Rom 12).

In a very real sense, it is possible that the future of the church is intricately tied to our treatment of people like Onesimus. He represents people on the margins who have been looked over, labeled, mistreated, ignored, and excluded. The irony of the letter is that these people are essential to the future and destiny of the church. Just as Philemon and the church in Colossae were better when Onesimus came back and was rightly recognized as a brother, so too are our churches better when we do the same. The church experiences spiritual impoverishment by trying to hold down, hold back, and silence the very people with the gifts to renew us. This is why, for example, the growth of the church in the two-thirds world is so promising for the future of the church. Like Onesimus, Christians in the two-thirds world have found the gospel outside of the "master's house" of Europe and North America. This could mean that the best chance for the revitalization of the church in North America may well come from a new global koinōnia with sisters and brothers who encountered Christ from a different place, and so, I encourage the church in North America to open its eyes, arms, and minds to the gifts they bring us.

Furthermore, there is a deeper and more relevant theological message here regarding the church's continued blindness to slavery and poverty because it sensitizes the church in a pastoral way that can help us. Maybe the greatest reason to delve deeply into the letter to Philemon and its message for the church today is that it will open our eyes to people who are locked into a modern form of slavery that supports criminal activities, immoral activities, and economically exploitative business practices. Slavery is still a real problem in the world today. There are close to 30 million people in various forms of slavery in the world today.[16] Many of the victims are women and children forced into sex trafficking, which is the third largest international crime industry (behind drugs and arms), generating $32 billion per year. We are blind to the millions of women and children trapped in the vicious tentacles of slavery. The longer they remain slaves, the less vital the church will be, because their gifts are locked away, their voices silenced. It

16. Fisher, "This Map."

would be thoroughly inappropriate to talk about sending these people back into situations of violence, exploitation, and other forms of harm. Until such systems are dismantled there can be no reconciliation. This does mean that the letter to Philemon is an invitation to reorient the witness of the church through the experiences of saints like Onesimus in ways that repudiate the continued practice of slavery and systems that keep billions of people mired in poverty. It also exposes the damaging effects of slavery on the witness of the church, blinding us to the plight of millions who experience the soul crushing despair of human enslavement in a world that celebrates freedom as a universal human right. The turn to Onesimus opens our eyes to those who experience abject poverty in a world with an abundance of material wealth and to those who experience dehumanization because of their gender. Onesimus can open our eyes to issues that the church universal shamefully ignores, keeping us spiritually wretched, miserable, poor, blind, and naked like the church of Laodicea (Rev 3:14–22).

I end my study of Philemon with a small hope that the church will look to Onesimus as the key to revitalization. I hope our denominations, institutions, and churches take up issues like slavery and global poverty in earnest and work to eradicate its presence in the world by leading moral campaigns against human trafficking, sweat shops, exploitative business practices, and the inequitable distribution of wealth. I earnestly believe the world will take note of such a Christian witness in a way that our singing and buildings will never do. In the end, perhaps the millions of Christians who previously left churches might return when they see a witness like the one Onesimus experienced in a prison cell with Paul. May it be, amen.

QUESTIONS FOR REFLECTION

1. What is koinōnia? Why is this word important? How does a person's understanding and practice of koinōnia affect the salvation of non-Christians like Onesimus and the sanctification of Christians? In what way is the letter to Philemon a challenge for the church to evaluate its understanding and, more importantly, its practice of koinōnia?

2. How does the exclusionary koinōnia theory influence the interpretation of the letter, opening the way for discussion on issues like racism, sexism, and classism in ways not possible with the slave flight theory?

Bibliography

Armstrong, George D. *The Christian Doctrine of Slavery*. Norfolk, VA: Charles Scribner, 1857.

Arndt, William, and F. Wilbur Gingrich. *A Greek English Lexicon of the New Testament*. 2nd ed. Translated by Walter Bauer. Chicago: University of Chicago Press, 1979.

Aquinas, Thomas. *Commentaries on St. Paul's Epistles to Timothy, Titus, and Philemon*. Translated by Chrysostom Baer. South Bend, IN: St. Augustine's, 2007.

Barclay, William. *The Letters to Timothy, Titus, and Philemon*. Philadelphia: Westminster, 1975.

———. "Paul, Philemon and the Dilemma of Christian Slave-Ownership." *New Testament Studies* 37 (1991) 161–86.

Barna, George. *Revolution*. Carol Stream, IL: Tyndale, 2012.

Barna, George, and David Kinnaman. *Churchless: Understanding Today's Unchurched and How to Connect With Them*. Carol Stream, IL: Tyndale Momentum, 2014.

Barnes, Albert. *An Inquiry Into the Scriptural Views of Slavery*. New York: Negro Universities Press, 1969.

Barth, Markus, and Helmut Blanke. *The Letter to Philemon*. Eerdmans Critical Commentary. Grand Rapids: Eerdmans, 2000.

Bieberstein, Sabine. "Disrupting the Normal Reality of Slavery: A Feminist Reading of the Letter to Philemon." *Journal for the Study of the New Testament* 79 (2000) 109–11.

Blass, William, and A. Debrunner. *Greek Grammar of the New Testament and Other Early Christian Literature*. Translated by Robert Funk. Chicago: University of Chicago Press, 1961.

Blount, Brian, et al., eds. *True to Our Native Land: An African American New Testament Commentary*. Minneapolis: Fortress, 2007.

Braxton, Brad. *The Tyranny of Resolution: 1 Corinthians 7:17–24.* Atlanta: Society of Biblical Literature, 2000.

Breasted, James Henry. *Ancient Times: A History of the Early World.* 2nd ed. Boston: Ginn and Co., 1935.

Brogdon, Lewis. *Dying to Lead.* Laurel, MD: Seymour, 2015.

————. "Exclusion as Impediment to Salvation: An African American Reading of Paul's Letter to Philemon." PhD diss., Regent University, 2010.

————. "Interpreting Pauline Slave Texts." Master's thesis, Louisville Presbyterian Theological Seminary, 2005.

Brown, Raymond. *An Introduction to the New Testament.* New York: Doubleday, 1997.

Bruce, F. F. *The Epistles to the Colossians, to Philemon and to the Ephesians.* New International Commentary of the New Testament. Grand Rapids: Eerdmans, 1984.

Caird, G. B. *New Testament Theology.* Edited by L. D. Hurst. New York: Oxford University Press, 1994.

Callahan, Allen D. *Embassy of Onesimus: The Letter of Paul to Philemon.* Valley Forge, PA: Trinity, 1997.

————. "John Chrysostom on Philemon: A Response to Margaret Mitchell." *Harvard Theological Review* 86 (1995) 149–50.

————. "Paul's Epistle to Philemon: Toward an Alternate Argumentum." *Harvard Theological Review* 86 (1993) 357–76.

Callahan, Allen D., et al. "Introduction: The Slavery of New Testament Studies." *Semia* 83–84 (1998) 1–11.

Calvin, John. *The Epistles of Paul to the Galatians and Ephesians.* Translated by William Pringle. Grand Rapids: Baker, 1981.

Church, F. Forrester. "Rhetorical Structure and Design in Paul's Letter to Philemon." *Harvard Theological Review* 71 (1978) 17–33.

Coleman-Norton, P. R. *Studies in Roman Economic and Social History.* Princeton: Princeton University Press, 1951.

Davis, Brion. *The Problem of Slavery in Western Culture.* New York: Cornell University Press, 1966.

De Vos, Craig. "Once a Slave, Always a Slave? Slavery, Manumission and Relational Patterns in Paul's Letter to Philemon." *Journal of the Study of the New Testament* 82 (2001) 89–105.

Dunn, James D. G. *The Epistles to the Colossians and to Philemon.* The New International Greek Testament Commentary. Grand Rapids: Eerdmans, 1996.

Felder, Cain Hope. *Stony the Road We Trod: African American Biblical Interpretation.* Minneapolis: Fortress, 2006.

Bibliography

Fisher, Max. "This Map Shows Where the World's 30 Million Slaves Live: There Are 60,000 in the U.S." *The Washington Post*, October 17, 2013. https://www.washingtonpost.com/news/worldviews/wp/2013/10/17/this-map-shows-where-the-worlds-30-million-slaves-live-there-are-60000-in-the-u-s/?utm_term=.d1f3db874abc.

Fitzmyer, Joseph. *The Letter to Philemon*. Anchor Bible Commentary 34C. New York: Doubleday, 2000.

Friedrich, Gerhard. *Theological Dictionary of the New Testament*. Translated by Geoffrey W. Bromiley. Grand Rapids: Eerdmans, 1971.

Garland, David. *Colossians, Philemon*. The NIV Application Commentary. Grand Rapids: Zondervan, 1998.

Getty, Mary Ann. "The Letter to Philemon." *The Bible Today* (May 1984) 137–44.

———. "The Theology of Philemon." *Society of Biblical Literature 1987 Seminar Papers* 26 (1987) 503–8.

Glancy, Jennifer. *Slavery in Early Christianity*. New York: Oxford University Press, 2002.

Hendriksen William. *New Testament Commentary*. Vol. 9, *Exposition of Colossians and Philemon*. Grand Rapids: Baker, 1979.

How, Samuel Blanchard. *Slaveholding Not Sinful*. New York: Books for Libraries, 1971.

Johnson, Luke Timothy. *The Writings of the New Testament: An Interpretation*. Minneapolis: Fortress, 1999.

Keck, Leander. *The New Interpreter's Bible*. Vol. 11. Nashville: Abingdon, 2000.

King, Martin Luther, Jr. *A Testament of Hope: The Essential Writings of Martin Luther King Jr*. Edited by James Melvin Washington. San Francisco: Harper and Row, 1986.

Kittel, Gerhard. *Theological Dictionary of the New Testament*. Vol. 3. Translated by Geoffrey Bromiley. Grand Rapids: Eerdmans, 1965.

Knox, John. *Philemon Among the Letters of Paul: A New View of Its Place and Importance*. Chicago: University of Chicago Press, 1935.

Koenig, John. *Philemon*. Augsburg Commentary on the New Testament. Minneapolis: Augsburg, 1985.

Lampe, Peter. "Keine Sklavenflucht des Onesimus." *Zeitschrift Fur Die Neutestamentliche Wissenschaft* 76 (1985) 135–37.

Bibliography

Lightfoot, J. B. *Colossians and Philemon*. Crossway Classic Commentaries. Edited by Alister McGrath and J. I. Packer. Wheaton, IL: Crossway, 1997.

Lightfoot, J. B., and J. R. Harner. *The Apostolic Fathers*. Berkeley: Apocryphile, 2004.

Lohse, Eduard. *Colossians and Philemon*. Translated by William Poehlmann and Robert J. Harris. Hermeneia. Philadelphia: Fortress, 1971.

Luther, Martin. *The Works of Martin Luther*. Translated by Jaroslav Pelikan. Philadelphia: A. J. Holman, 1982.

Lyons, K. D. "Paul's Confrontation with Class. The Letter to Philemon as Counter-Hegemonic Discourse." *Cross Currents* 55 (2005) 322–39.

Martin, Clarice. "The Rhetorical Function of Commercial Language in Paul's Letter to Philemon (Verse 18)." In *Persuasive Artistry: Studies in New Testament Rhetoric in Honor of George A. Kennedy*, edited by Duane F. Watson, 321–37. JSNT Supplement Series 50. Sheffield, JSOT, 1991.

———. "Somebody Done Hoodoo'd the Hodoo Man: Language, Power, Resistance, and the Effective History of Pauline Texts in American Slavery." *Semeia* 83–84 (1998) 203–33.

Martin, Dale. *Slavery as Salvation: The Metaphor of Slavery in Pauline Christianity*. New York: Oxford University Press, 2002.

Mayes, James L. *HarperCollins Bible Commentary*. San Francisco: HarperCollins, 2000.

Mitchell, Margaret. "John Chrysostom on Philemon." *Harvard Theological Review* 88 (1995) 135–38.

Moo, Douglas. *The Letters to the Colossians and to Philemon*. The Pillar New Testament Commentary. Grand Rapids: Eerdmans, 2008.

Nordling, John G. "Onesimus Fugitivus: A Defense of the Runaway Slave Hypothesis in Philemon." *Journal of the Study of the New Testament* 41 (Feb 1981) 97–119.

———. *Philemon*. Concordia Commentary. St. Louis: Concordia, 2004.

O'Brien, Peter T. *Colossians and Philemon*. Word Biblical Commentary 44. Dallas: Word Books, 1982.

Olson, David T. *The American Church in Crisis*. Grand Rapids: Zondervan, 2008.

Patterson, Orlando. *Slavery and Social Death*. Cambridge: Harvard University Press, 1982.

Pavlovitz, John. "Church, Here's Why People Are Leaving You, Part 1." *Stuff That Needs to be Said* (blog), August 15, 2014. https://

Bibliography

johnpavlovitz.com/2014/08/15/church-heres-why-people-are-leaving-you-part-1/.

Priest, Josiah. *Bible Defence of Slavery*. Glasgow, KY: Rev W. S. Brown, 1853.

Raboteau, Albert. *Slave Religion: The Invisible Institution in the Antebellum South*. New York: Oxford University Press, 2004.

Rapske, Brian M. "The Prisoner Paul in the Eyes of Onesimus." *New Testament Studies* 37 (1991) 187–203.

Sanders, Laura L. "Equality and a Request for the Manumission of Onesimus." *Restoration Quarterly* (n.d.) 109–14.

Schaff, Philip. *Nicene and Post-Nicene Fathers*. Vol. 13. Peabody, MA: Hendrickson, 1995.

Seneca. "On Master and Slave." In *Epistulae Morales*, translated by Richard Gummere. Loeb Classical Library. Cambridge: Harvard University Press, 1917.

Sernett, Milton C. *African American Religious History: A Documentary Witness*. Durham: Duke University Press, 1999.

Soards, Marion. "Some Neglected Theological Dimensions of Paul's Letter to Philemon." *Perspectives in Religious Studies* (1990) 209–20.

Spong, John Shelby. *The Sins of Scripture*. San Francisco: Harper Collins, 2005.

Stuart, Moses. *Conscience and Constitution*. Boston: Crocker and Brewster, 1850.

Stuhlmacher, Peter. *Der Brief an Philemon*. Evangelisch-Katholischer Kommentar zum Neuen Testament. Benziger: Verlag, 1989.

Thompson, Joseph. *The Fugitive Slave Law Tried by the Old and New Testament*. New York: Mark H. Newman and Co., 1850. https://archive.org/details/fugitiveslavelawoothom.

Tidball, Derek. *The Social Context of the New Testament: A Sociological Analysis*. Grand Rapids: Academie Books, 1984.

Van Dyke, Robert H. "Paul's Letter to Philemon: An Appeal Above and Beyond the Law." *Sewanee Theological Review* 4 (1998) 384–98.

Vincent, Marvin. *Philippians and Philemon*. The International Critical Commentary. Edinburgh: T & T Clark, 1955.

Weld, Theodore. *The Bible Against Slavery*. New York: American Anti-Slavery Society, 1837.

Westermann, William L. *The Slave Systems of Greek and Roman Antiquity*. Philadelphia: American Philosophical Society, 1955.

Wilson, Robert. *Colossians and Philemon*. International Critical Commentary. New York: T&T Clark, 2005.

Winter, Sarah C. "Methodological Observations in a New Interpretation of Paul's Letter to Philemon." *Union Seminary Quarterly* 39 (1984) 203–12.

———. "Paul's Letter to Philemon." *New Testament Studies* 33 (Jan 1987) 1–15.

Younger, Pliny the. *Epistles.* Translated by William Melmoth. Loeb Classical Library. Cambridge: Harvard University Press, 1915.